TURKEY

LIVE & WORK in...

TURKEY

Comprehensive,
up-to-date,
practical
information about
everyday life

HUW FRANCIS

howto**books**

How To Books Ltd
Spring Hill House, Spring Hill Road
Begbroke, Oxford OX5 1RX, United Kingdom
Tel: 01865 375794 Fax: 01865 379162
info@howtobooks.co.uk
www.howtobooks.co.uk

The right of Huw Francis to be identified as author of this work has been
asserted by him in accordance with the Copyright, Design and Patents Act 1988.

British Library Cataloguing in Publication Data
A catalogue record for this book is available from
the British Library.

First published 2008

ISBN: 978 1 84528 245 5

Cover design by Baseline Arts
Produced for How To Books by Deer Park Productions, Tavistock
Typeset by *specialist* publishing services ltd, Montgomery
Printed and bound by Cromwell Press, Trowbridge, Wiltshire

Contents

Foreword

Living and/or working abroad is a dream for many people. Gone are the days, however, when you had to run away to sea to explore the world. The global economy has changed the way the world works and opened up many more opportunities.

Whether you take a gap year, become a teacher, follow an international career in business, or go it alone and set up your own business in a foreign country, there are many ways and places to live internationally whilst working.

France, Italy and Spain have long been popular retirement destinations with Britons, Europeans and North Americans, but as the traditional retirement destinations have become old hat and swamped with foreign retirees, other destinations have become more interesting.

From long before Agatha Christie wrote *Murder On The Orient Express*, there has been a romanticised image of Turkey that was probably never quite true to reality. Many people avoided Turkey because of its disreputable reputation, but the brave few who visited for some excitement generally found they had a great time in a beautiful country and were welcomed with open arms by the hospitable Turks.

With a cultural heritage to match, or even outdo, Greece and Italy, Turkey is where much of what we know of as classical history actually took place. Ephesus, Troy, Aphrodite, King Midas, Constantinople, Trebizond, Byzantium and Mount Ararat are all part of Turkey's rich history.

As the seat of two major religions, Constantinople was a powerful city at the time of the Ottoman Empire. Both the Caliphate and Patriarchy of the Eastern Orthodox Church called it home and the city was also a haven for

European Jews and a large Armenian population well into the twentieth century.

Politically it is unique. As a secular, multi-party, republican democracy this is a Muslim country where the military has intervened in politics a number of times to protect democracy from Communism and Islamism. However, full membership of the European Union has been an aspiration for decades and this would complement Turkey's membership of the UN, NATO, OECD and other international organisations.

Economically Turkey has grown significantly in the last 15 years, despite a few years of economic turmoil caused by high inflation and a large earthquake. As an associate member of the EU, the customs union with Europe has boosted the manufacturing industry and large numbers of motor vehicles and electronic goods are exported to Europe as well as Asia and the Middle East. Textiles, construction and the financial sector are all major contributors to the economy, as is tourism, which has underpinned much of Turkey's economic growth. Capital expenditure on major infrastructure projects has also boosted the economy and further benefited the manufacturing sectors.

As the stereotypical crossroads of Europe and Asia, the country also has a wonderfully varied cuisine drawing on Mediterranean, Asian and Middle Eastern influences. As you travel around the country the variation in the local delicacies will keep any serious gastronome in raptures, though a wine connoisseur will need time to find some wines to their taste out of the many produced from the hundreds of native vines.

Active types will have plenty to keep them occupied too. With skiing, sailing, climbing and trekking within easy reach of most areas, weekends, short breaks and longer holidays are well catered for. Football is the most popular spectator sport, as well as being widely played at amateur level, and some of the more successful club teams compete well in European competitions, as does the international side on the world stage.

Today, Ankara is the political capital, with Istanbul being the commercial capital. Antalya and Bodrum would probably argue about which is the tourism capital. As an international city, Istanbul attracts its share of well-travelled expatriates as well as newly-qualified teachers of English as a foreign language (TEFL) wanting to work and travel. Ankara, Izmir and some of the other larger cities experience smaller numbers of working travellers. The tourist areas also attract foreign residents, though here they often split into two types – retirees and tourism entrepreneurs.

As a place to live, Turkey still offers a true cultural experience. You know you are in Turkey from the moment you get off the plane, train or boat. It is not the place for someone looking for a home away from home with northern European foodstuffs on every corner. This is not the Costa del Sol of Spain; even on the tourist-swamped coast near Bodrum you cannot forget you are in Turkey.

Though the country has one foot in Europe and one in Asia, it has its own culture that is markedly different from both. Culture shock hits most foreign residents and can be too much for some to cope with, but for those who prepare for their move and make the effort to understand what is happening around them, Turkey is a rewarding experience that will more than repay the effort put into enjoying it.

1
Introducing Turkey

HISTORY

The modern Republic of Turkey (Turkiye Çumhuriyet) officially came
into being on October 29th, 1923. The first president was Mustafa Kemal
Atatürk, a successful general who had fought with distinction in the First
World War and against the various armies (Greece, France, Italy, Britain)
who invaded or occupied parts of Turkey in the years to 1923. His legacy
still dominates the country's consciousness and political system.

Despite its relative youth as a country, the geopolitical predecessors of the
current state of Turkey have left a rich and complex cultural, religious and
political history that impacts on the current country and its immediate
neighbours, as well as on the wider world.

Classical History

Many of the myths and legends of the ancient world are often centred on
Turkey. Jason led his Argonauts along the Black Sea coast to Trebizond
(Trabzon) looking for the Golden Fleece. The flames of the Chimaera still
break the surface of the ground near Antalya on Mount Olympos. And the
wonders of Troy are to be found on the western coast of Turkey.

Archaeological digs have revealed finds dating back to the palaeolithic
age. The neolithic settlement at Çatalhöyük, south of Konya, was founded
in 6500BC – a site still remarkably well preserved today. The following

I

8,500 years of history in the region cover much of what we know as classical history and defined the modern world. The names of historical rulers, civilisations and places are well known to people all over the world and are part of the English speaking world's heritage as much as they are of Turkey's.

The names of Croesus, King Midas, Alexander the Great and St Paul, the Hittites, Galatians and Phrygians and the cities of Troy, Gordion, Constantinople and Antioch are all well known, though few people realise their place in Turkish history.

Agamemnon and the wars with Troy are included in the *Iliad* and took place on the coast of what is now Turkey. The Phrygians were one of the earliest civilisations of Turkey and the golden touch of King Midas in his city of Gordion have remained in our folklore. Gordion lies an hour west of Ankara on the Anatolian plains and Midas' massive tomb, one of many tumuli at Gordion, demonstrates the power and wealth he must have commanded in 700BC.

Croesus also ruled at a similar time to Midas, but over the Lydians, until the Persians invaded and pushed the Lydian civilisation aside. Having introduced the idea of using coins as currency, Croesus gave his name to the saying, 'As rich as Croesus'.

When the Persians invaded and subjugated the Ionian cities that gave the world their majestic Ionic Columns, the Hellenistic culture of what is now Turkey went into decline. However, just too far away for the Persians to occupy successfully, Athens began its ascent as the centre of Hellenism.

Alexander the Great overwhelmed the Persians when he swept out of Macedonia in 300BC, before he went on to conquer the Middle East and reach India. As he crossed Turkey he cut the Gordion Knot at Gordium then gave his Macedonian name, Iskender, to the city of Iskenderun and left his name on a particularly delicious Turkish dish, the Iskender Kebab.

After Alexander, the Celts arrived and made their Galatian capital at what is now Ankara. The Armenians also settled in the east of the country and the great kingdom of Pergamum began its rise to power.

The Romans

The Romans arrived next: they moved into western Turkey and inherited most of Anatolia when the last Pergamum king died without an heir and left his kingdom to Rome.

The pre-Christian rulers of Turkey also left a number of monuments on the landscape that remain to this day. Mausolus left his tomb, the Mausoleum, at Halicarnassus (Bodrum) and Antiochus left a temple and huge stone heads at Nemrut Dağ. The Pontic kings left magnificent rock-carved tombs at Amasya and there are Lycian tombs in the sea cliffs near Dalyan.

Once Christianity arrived it made a massive impression on the country. St Paul, from Tarsus on the south east coast of Turkey, brought back Christianity and preached at Ephesus, where he wrote his letter to the Ephesians. The Seven Churches of Revelation are all in Turkey (Ephesus, Smyrna, Pergamum, Sardis, Philadelphia, Thyatira and Laodicea). Cappadocia and Phrygia are also mentioned in the bible and the house of Mary, the Mother of Jesus, is on a hill near Ephesus. The first three Ecumenical Councils of Churches were also held in Turkey, at Nicea in 325, Constantinople in 381 and Ephesus in 431.

As the western Roman Empire in Europe crumbled under assault from the Goths and Vandals, the eastern empire regrouped, grew richer and built New Rome at Byzantium, which then went on to become Constantinople.

The Romans brought peace and roads, as well as wealth and magnificent buildings. Roman remains litter modern Turkey and have survived well in the dry heat of Anatolia. So well, in fact, that the last will and testament of Augustus Caesar can still be read where it was engraved on the walls of the Temple of Augustus and Rome in Ankara.

The Islamic Empire

As the Roman Empire declined under weakening emperors, the Muslim Arabic Empire grew outward from Medina. At its peak, the Islamic Empire stretched from western Turkey to Iran and into Egypt.

Mohammed's successors, the Caliphs, ruled over a period of great cultural achievement for almost 500 years. During this time the Turks, from central Asia, were employed as mercenaries and were a major factor in the Arabic empire's successes.

The Turkish Selçuk Empire

The Turks eventually became too powerful to be controlled and the Turkish Selçuk Empire established itself in Persia. The Selçuk army moved west and took Baghdad, before squeezing the Byzantines westwards and taking over Anatolia. The distinctive Selçuk architecture graces many mosques in today's Turkey and their greatest poet, Omar Khayyam, gave the world his *Rubaiyat*.

When the Selçuk Empire declined, it split into Sultanates, with Anatolia going its own way. During this Selçuk period the Mevlana established the mystic order of the Whirling Dervishes. Having grown to hold significant political power they were expelled to Konya by Atatürk and stripped of much of their influence.

A mostly uncharted period of Turkish history followed, when the Mongols charged in, leaving only a few buildings and little else when they left in a little over 100 years. Huge numbers of Turkic refugees fled westward across Anatolia in front of the Mongols, pushing up against the Byzantine Empire. As they went westward and fought a rearguard action against the Mongols, the Turks learnt to use the cavalry techniques of the invader. This horsemanship they put to good use against the Byzantines, and later for the Byzantine Empire as mercenaries. Though the Mongols reached beyond present day Ankara, they never completely took over the region.

While the weakening remains of the Byzantine Empire faced the fractured remains of the Selçuk Empire, they also had to contend with four crusades of European Christians heading off to liberate the Holy Land. Christian Constantinople was even invaded and pillaged by one of these crusades.

The minor Selçuk Turk fiefdoms took advantage of the weakened Byzantine Empire and picked off their lands piecemeal. Though they captured most of Anatolia and grouped around the chieftain Osman, who gave his name to the Osmanlı (Ottoman) Empire, Constantinople remained a Christian Byzantine city.

The Ottoman Empire

Constantinople finally fell to the Ottomans in 1453 and they moved into Europe, through the Balkans, over the next 80 years. By this time the Ottoman Empire stretched from the Arabian Peninsula to Austria and rivalled the great Empires of history.

As with most great Empires, it fell into a long and slow decline. In the case of the Ottoman Empire the decline took 300 years to really bite and Greece did not gain full independence until 1832, though it declared independence in 1822. Once the breakup started, it accelerated and the Balkan states gained independence soon after Greece.

The major powers of the time saw the chance to add to their own Empires and Britain, France, Germany and Russia all manœuvred for influence, power and land, and eventually came to blows in the Crimean War of the 1850s.

The Young Turks

With the Sultanate intent on modernising without democracy, a young generation of Turks grew increasingly frustrated until the Young Turks took power in parliament in 1908 and then replaced the Sultan with his brother in 1909.

A committee of three Young Turks ruled the country from then on and, disastrously, they joined with Germany in the First World War. With the defeat of Germany and its allies, the victorious parties divided up the remains of the Ottoman Empire between them. Britain occupied Constantinople, Italy and France landed on the Mediterranean coast and Greece invaded at Smyrna (Izmir).

Mustafa Kemal and Modernisation

To the surprise of many, the Turks rallied under the leadership of General Mustafa Kemal, who had led the defence against the British at the Battle of Gallipoli in the First World War. Though the Greek army moved to within reach of Ankara, the Turkish army won the Battle of Sakarya in 1921 and the tide of history began to turn in Turkey's favour. The Greek army retreated, burning everything behind them and the city of Smyrna burnt to the ground – though both sides dispute who was responsible for the destruction of the city.

In 1923 the Republic of Turkey was formally proclaimed and Mustafa Kemal began his task of remodelling an entire country.

The impact of Kemal Atatürk on Turkey should never be underestimated. His image adorns office walls and public buildings and many official publications. He set out to rebuild Turkey as a modern European nation that could take its place on the world stage with none of the baggage associated with the Ottoman Empire and made a huge impact on the country in a relatively short time.

Atatürk did not do anything by halves. He secularised the country with an official separation of state from religion. He abolished the sharia courts and introduced a civil code based on Swiss law. The *fez* was banned. A new phonetic alphabet was developed by European linguists to replace the Arabic script so that literacy rates could be improved. International time and calendar systems were adopted to replace the Islamic calendar.

Change swept Turkey along on a road to westernisation, then Atatürk died in 1938 only fifteen years after the founding of the state of Turkey. As subsequent politicians tried to outdo each other to be more Kemalist than the next, the pace of change slowed and arguments raged over whether Atatürk would have approved of further changes.

Despite the population being predominantly Muslim, the secularisation of government is strictly enforced; the wearing of head scarves is forbidden in public buildings, for example, and relaxation of this law only began in 2008. However, there is freedom of religious practice but, though not actually forbidden, attempting to change people's religious beliefs is seriously frowned upon.

Atatürk's ruling Republican Party has always been to the right of the political scale, but social and political Islam has, however, always been present in Turkey. There have been three military coups (1960, 1971 and 1980) that brought down leftist or Islamic governments. There was also a soft coup in 1997 when Necmettin Erbakan, leader of the Welfare Party, who was banned from politics after the 1980 coup until 1990, was forced to resign when the army publicly warned him about his pro-Islamic pronouncements and the tanks rolled through the streets of the Ankara suburb of Sincan.

The army constitution demands that it protects Turkey's secularism and it does so with vigour. Military rule after each coup has always been short, with the army pushing the country back to democracy as soon as it can.

This interventionist policy, though, has led to problems with Turkey's accession to the European Union. Having first applied for membership in 1957, an association agreement was signed in 1963. A full application was then submitted in 1987, but turned down in 1989. Turkey finally signed a customs union in 1995 and was recognised as a candidate for full membership in 1997. Membership talks, however, only began in 2005 and are likely to be long and slow.

Turkish politics have always been volatile and this looks unlikely to change in the foreseeable future.

RELIGION

Islam

Sitting between the Muslim Arab countries and Christian Europe, modern Turkey is Islamic by religion, but home to the Eastern Orthodox Church and has been a refuge for Jews fleeing persecution for many hundreds of years.

Mostly Sunni, the Muslim population is around 98% of the overall population of the country. With its rich religious history, the historic mosques that dot the country are a reminder of the days when Islam was a progressive and dynamic driver for change in the region.

Despite being a staunchly secular government, a large number of new mosques have been built by the religious affairs department and in most towns and villages there are numerous shiny white minarets piercing the skyline.

The middle class Turks are often relaxed about their religion and only visit the mosque for special occasions, much like many middle class Britons visiting church at Easter and Christmas. Alcohol is widely drunk and cigarettes are cheap and smoked almost continuously and it is not uncommon for Turkish friends to say they will give up alcohol and cigarettes for Ramadan.

However, political Islam has been a constant presence in the country and a minority would like to see an Islamic Republic, similar to to that found in Iran. This has caused political unrest as the secular and religious parties vie for power and dominance. Army intervention in politics has happened four times since the Second World War and has always been to protect the secularist state from a perceived Islamic threat.

Judaism

There is a sizeable Jewish population in Turkey which was first established over 2,000 years ago, though the current population was established in 1492 when Spain expelled its Jewish population. Sultan Beyazit welcomed the Spanish Jews and started a tradition of tolerance and welcome to the Jewish community.

In 1933 Atatürk invited Jewish professors suffering persecution in Germany to the universities of Turkey and in the 1940s rescued over 100,000 Jews from France and Eastern Europe.

Though the Jewish population has declined from its peak in the early 20th century, there are still synagogues in Ankara, Izmir, Bursa and Istanbul.

Christianity

Despite having once been the official religion of the Byzantine Empire as well as home to significant populations of refugee Christians in the early years following the death of Christ, Christianity is not a common religion in modern day Turkey.

There are several churches in the big cities, as well as the pilgrimage sites of Ephesus, the seven Churches of Revelation and the house of Mary the Mother of Jesus among others. These, however, attract mainly western tourists and expatriates living in Turkey.

The head of the Eastern Orthodox Church (Ecumenical Patriarchate of Constantinople) is also based in Istanbul, the traditional home of the Greek Orthodox Church. Since the treaty of Lausanne in 1923 and the exchange of populations between Greece and Turkey, the Greek Christian community in Istanbul has sharply declined.

PEOPLE

Officially, the population of Turkey is 100% Turkish. This is a technical description for all Turkish nationals as there are sizeable ethnic communities scattered around the country. The Turks themselves were the last of a long line of invaders who stayed in the country, the Mongols came later, but left again.

While the Selçuks and later the Ottomans ruled the country, the existing tribes stayed and maintained their identities into modern times.

There are communities of ethnic Greeks, Armenians, Kurds and Laz. These communities are Muslim, but still have their own languages, concentrated in the east of Anatolia and often form the majority of the population in their respective areas.

POLITICS

Since the formation of the Republic of Turkey in 1923, the country has been a secular democracy. However, there have been extended periods of one-party rule in the early days of the Republic, three coups (1960, 1971 and 1980) and two interventions (1997 and 2007) by the military.

Since the last coup of 1980, Turkey has seen a rise in left of centre political Islam that has competed successfully with the more right wing Republicanism of the traditional parties. In 1996 the Refah (Welfare) Party entered power in a coalition government and in the 2002 election the left-leaning Islamist Justice and Development (AK) Party won a landslide victory.

Both of the Islamist governments (1996 and 2002) have faced severe pressure from the military not to implement policies seen as undermining the secular state. In 1997 Neçmettin Erbakan was forced to resign as Prime Minister after the army drove its tanks through the streets of an Ankara suburb. In 2007 Abdullah Gül was forced to withdraw his nomination for President following parliamentary boycotts, high court judgements, massive demonstrations and strong criticism from the military.

To complicate the matter, the middle class cities are usually staunch supporters of the secular state and the poor and rural areas more likely to support the Islamic parties.

Notably, the army considers itself the guardian of the secular democratic system and has always swiftly returned the country to civilian rule after its coups.

Despite its perceived Islamist roots, the AK Party is pro-Europe and has driven through many reforms to help Turkey's application for EU membership.

In addition to the rise of political Islam, the political and cultural aspirations of the Kurdish minority in south east Turkey have re-emerged since the early 1980s. Discontent with what they saw as oppression of their cultural identity, the Kurdistan Workers' Party (Partiya Karkere Kurdistan – PKK) was formed in 1984 and began what became a violent and bloody fight for independence from Turkey.

In parallel, though closely linked to the PKK, a number of political parties have emerged in the south east and gained significant representation in the National Assembly. The close links with the PKK have resulted in some of the parties being disbanded by the courts and some Kurdish MPs being imprisoned for 'crimes against the state'. As the military sought to restore peace in the south east, many Kurds arrived as refugees from Iraq and others moved to western Turkey to escape the violence.

Following the arrest of the leader of the PKK, Abdullah Öçalan, a ceasefire came into force and calm returned, the ceasefire has since broken down and new bombings and other attacks have occurred in parts of Turkey previously free from violence.

Greater freedoms have been given to the Kurds of Turkey, but the Turkish government is still fearful that they seek further autonomy, or independence. The increased autonomy of the Iraqi Kurdish region has further alarmed the Turkish administration and the repeated military incursions by the Turkish army into Iraq highlight their concerns.

On the world stage, Turkey is a member of NATO and the OECD, as well as the Black Sea Economic Cooperation Organization, Islamic Conference Association, the UN and the European Council. As a democratic and predominantly Muslim country Turkey's influence in the Middle East is sought by other world leaders, though Turkey is increasingly seeking to determine its own place in the world.

GOVERNMENT

Turkey is a multi-party, secular, parliamentary democracy. There are 550 representatives voted into parliament for a five-year term and a government is formed by the largest party, or a coalition of parties. The Prime Minister is the leader of the ruling group and the Head of Government, who is appointed by the President.

Legislative power rests with the government, and the parliament is known as the Grand National Assembly of Turkey (Türkiye Büyük Millet Meclisi). The Prime Minister appoints his ministers to the ruling cabinet and the Assembly has traditionally elected the President, who may, or may not, be a member of parliament as is seen fit. In 2007 the ruling AK Party introduced legislation for the President to be elected by the people.

Compared with Britain there are many parties represented in the Turkish parliament and it is not uncommon for MPs to change party allegiance after election and for parties to merge, split, disappear, or be banned by the courts. A number of currently prominent politicians have previously been banned from participating in political life, only having the bans lifted after long periods and court action.

In 2007 two parties dominated parliament, The Republican People's Party (CHP) and the Justice and Development (AK) Party. Eight independents completed the roster of MPs. Another 16 parties had also competed unsuccessfully in the election of 2002, a number of which had previously been represented and even been part of a ruling coalition.

Turkey is divided into 76 provinces (*vilayetlar*) and the Council of Ministers appoints a governor (*vagi*) to each, who oversees implementation of government policy. The provinces are subdivided into districts (*kazalar*) and sub-districts (*bucaklar*).

Regional assemblies (*vilayet genel meclisi*) are elected on a provincial basis and, under the direction of the governor, appoint committees to oversee the administration of the province. District chiefs (*kaymakam*) oversee a local council and supervise local government officials on behalf of the governor. District chiefs are appointed by the President after nomination from the Interior Minister.

Cities and towns with a population over 2,000 are classed as a municipality (*belediye*) and are governed by an elected mayor (*belediye reisi*). Elected municipal councils oversee the running of the municipality and promotions of local officials.

Sub-district chiefs (*bucak mudur*) are appointed by the Interior Minister after nomination by the Provincial Governor. They are responsible for local law and order in conjunction with other civil agencies.

The Civil Service set up in the 1920s and 1930s was loyal to Kemal Atatürk and as the National Assembly became increasingly democratic it resisted change perceived as anti-Kemalist. This led to tensions between the new political parties and the Civil Service, which came to a head after the coup of 1980 when the military introduced major reforms to make the Civil Service less independent and more under the control of the government.

Civil Servants cannot be members of a political party and must resign from the Civil Service if they wish to stand for election to public office.

The Judiciary is independent of the Government and the legal system was created by drawing on the laws of Switzerland, France, Germany, Italy and the UK.

There are various levels within the Turkish court system including the Constitutional Court (Anayasa Mahkemesi – www.anayasa.gov.tr), Supreme Court of Appeal (Yargitay Baskanligi – www.yargitay.gov.tr), Council of State (Danistay Ihlamur – www.danistay.gov.tr) and Court of Accounts (Sayistay Baskanligi – www.sayistay.gov.tr). As part of its ambitions towards EU membership, Turkey has joined the European Court of Human Rights and is a signatory of the European Convention on Human Rights.

ECONOMY

The health of the economy in Turkey has fluctuated wildly over the past 20 years. There have been periods of sustained high growth, as well as some major recessions. On the whole, however, the Turkish economy has grown significantly during the period and has developed greater stability in recent years.

Strong action by the government since the low periods of 1999 and 2001, in conjunction with the World Bank, has seen inflation fall, growth stabilise, exports grow and the New Turkish Lira (Yeni Turkçe Lira, YTL) remain stable on the foreign exchange markets.

The Customs Union with the EU in 1996 has resulted in good growth in exports, with a number of well known multi-national companies setting up operations in Turkey to take advantage of the skilled, but relatively cheap workforce and reduced tariffs on goods entering Europe. As the Customs

Union only applies to industrial and processed agricultural goods, Turkey's raw agricultural produce, such as olive oil, falls outside the agreement.

As part of Turkey's plans for further integration with Europe it has a number of trade agreements, mirroring the European Free Trade Area, to enhance its trading opportunities. Turkey is also amending its commercial law so that it more closely matches Europe in areas such as competition, intellectual property rights and international trading rules.

Since the 1980s Turkey has been privatising state owned companies and opening up the economy to international investors, which has increased the value of such privatisations.

Growing demand for imports by the increasingly wealthy population has meant that Turkey has a high trade deficit in goods, though tourism revenue goes some way towards compensating for this.

As the economy has matured, the traditional dependence on agriculture has declined, though it still represents a significant percentage of GDP. Per capita income has risen significantly, but at approximately US$5,000 is much lower that the European average.

Manufacturing Industry

The automotive sector is important, with manufacturers such as Ford, Mercedes, Fiat, Honda, Isuzu, Hyundai and BMC all producing vehicles in the country, alongside indigenous truck, bus and car producers. In addition there over 100 automotive component suppliers supporting the manufacturers who produce almost 1,000,000 vehicles annually in Turkey, of which around 60% are exported.

Production of white goods is also significant, with Turkey producing huge numbers of fridges, washing machines and televisions with which they often dominate the European market.

The textile sector, including clothes and traditional carpets, is also important and many European retailers source their products from the Denizli region in the south.

Industrial machinery, electronics, iron and steel, chemicals, shipbuilding and ceramics (traditional and modern) also play an important part in the Turkish economy and employ many thousands.

Service Sector

In the service sector, construction leads the way. Turkish firms have won significant contracts throughout the Middle East and North Africa, the former Soviet republics and increasingly in Europe. Turkish contractors proudly claim to have worked in over 60 countries and earned US$70 billion in international contracts. Turkish expertise and contacts have also proved useful in joint ventures helping European countries enter Central Asian markets.

Turkish exports reached US$73 billion in 2005, with 64% going to Europe, with Germany, the UK and Italy taking almost half of that. The USA, France, Spain, Iraq, Holland and Russia are also significant markets.

Tourism

As a tourist destination Turkey has few rivals. The sheer number of historical sites, the seemingly unending coastline, reliable weather, great food and competitive prices have brought tourists flocking to the country. In 2005 the figure broke the 21 million figure and generated more than US$18 billion in revenue.

The government is keen to promote the sector and encourages foreign investment in tourism; it has developed plans to build and sell one million properties, as second homes to foreign nationals. Special interest tourism is encouraged by the authorities, including eco-tourism, adventure sports, religious tours and cultural tours.

Germany, Russia, the UK, the Netherlands and Bulgaria account for more than half of the total tourists and these countries are keen investors in the sector.

Banking

Underpinning the economy is the banking sector, now overseen by the Banking Regulation and Supervision Agency (Bankacilik Düzenleme ve Denetleme Kurumu – BDDK). Since the financial crisis of 2001 the banking sector has been overhauled and regulatory oversight tightened up.

Turkish and international banks operate in the sector, with many well-known names sitting alongside their Turkish counterparts, and operate within international standards. Most banks in Turkey are members of the Society for Worldwide Interbank Financial Telecommunications (SWIFT) and the regional processing centre is in Istanbul.

Commercial banking products, including insurance, factoring and leasing are all available, alongside access to capital markets. The Turkish Stock Exchange has performed well in recent years and has risen by 500% since 2000.

GEOGRAPHY AND REGIONS

Turkey is famous for bridging Europe and Asia, but in reality the change is not as marked as would appear when standing on the shores of the Bosphorus. The population is not homogeneous, the landscape of this vast country varies enormously and the way of life of its inhabitants is hugely disparate from region to region.

There are ethnic Turks living as far west as Greece and as far north as Kosovo and Bosnia. There are Greek and Jewish communities in Istanbul, and by the time you reach Turkey's eastern borders the population includes Kurds, Arabs and Laz.

Having only come into being in 1923, Turkey was created from the remains of the Ottoman Empire. It had never really existed in history and its creation also involved an exchange of populations with its close neighbour Greece as well as an assimilation of ethnic groups within the newly defined borders into the new Turkish identity.

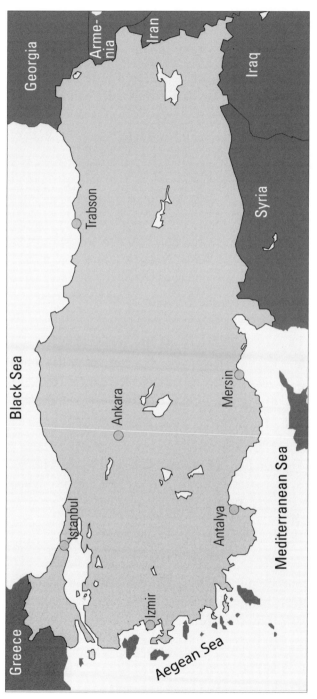

Present-day Turkey

Though modern Turkey is split into 76 provinces, the broader regions are more limited.

- There is European Turkey bordering Greece and Bulgaria, often known as Thrace. Jutting out of its south eastern extremity, into the Sea of Marmara, is the Gelibolu (Gallipoli) Peninsula.

- Istanbul is a region of its own and is home to many millions of people. It is the only city in the world to span two continents.

- The Aegean coast, running south from the Dardanelles, is a coastal plain with a number of major cities as well as important industry and fertile agricultural land. It includes the large area to the south of the Sea of Marmara.

- The Mediterranean coast stretches for many hundreds of kilometres towards the border with Arabic Syria past industrial towns, tourism hotspots and the oil terminal at Çeyhan.

- The Black Sea coast spans the north of the country from the Bosphorus to Georgia. Its damp climate and relative isolation make it green and fertile, producing tea and hazelnuts in abundance.

- Central Anatolia sits on a plateau in the centre of the country and is known as the breadbasket of Turkey. Fiercely cold in winter and burning hot in summer, it is a harsh and unforgiving region.

- The South East is rugged, mountainous and home to the Kurds, with their cultural capital in the city of Diyarbakir.

- Eastern Anatolia is sparsely populated and its population is a mix of the Kurds, Armenians and Turks living in isolated communities.

European Turkey

As a corridor into Asia and a route south from the Balkans to the Aegean Sea, Thrace has been fought over and changed hands many times. Since 1923 the borders have remained settled, despite the occupation of Greece by Germany in the Second World War.

Turkish Thrace (Trakya) is rarely visited by tourists, unless they are passing through on the route between Istanbul and Greece. It remains mostly rural, producing tobacco, silk and apricots among other less exotic products.

The main city is Edirne, a former Ottoman capital city, which was originally founded by the Emperor Hadrian. The border city boasts some fine Ottoman mosques and grand buildings as well as shady parks bordering the two rivers passing through it.

The other small towns of Thrace boast impressive mosques and *caravanserais* (quadrangular buildings erected to house travelling caravans), but without the tourists of their more well-known counterparts. To the south, on the shores of the Sea of Marmara, the town of Tekirdağ sits on the gentle hills that produce the grapes for its famous wines.

This rural idyll could soon change. Natural gas has been found under the soil and its exploitation could well change the landscape and pace of life significantly.

There is little that draws tourists to Thrace, except Gallipoli on the south west point, but this is a major pilgrimage point for young Australians and New Zealanders. The Dardanelles have been key to the protection of Istanbul for centuries, because if a navy was able to breach the defences, then Istanbul was open to attack.

In the First World War a naval attack failed to break through, so Churchill decided to send in the troops at Gallipoli in the north and Çannakkale on the south of the Dardenelle straits. Fierce fighting saw close to 100,000 men die and 400,000 more wounded. Both sides fought to a standstill, but the Turkish troops prevented a breakthrough and saved Istanbul. It was the battle where Atatürk made his name and he started his journey to become leader of the country.

The carnage of Gallipoli is marked with 31 cemeteries and every year thousands of people arrive to commemorate the dead, especially Australians and Kiwis, who remember the thousands of their comrades who fell at this famous First World War battlefield.

Istanbul

Istanbul could be a country in its own right. Its population certainly exceeds that of many nations and there is enough history and culture here to keep you occupied for years. Just listing all the names and stories of history that are associated with the place would fill many pages.

From its time as Byzantium, the city has been famous throughout the world. Supposedly founded on the advice of the Oracle of Delphi, the city has been a prize to be fought over and a power base to defend. Today, parts of the old town are UNESCO World Heritage sites, it will be the European Capital of Culture in 2010 and it is one of the world's largest cities with a population in the region of 15 million people.

It is no longer a political capital city, but it is the economic and cultural capital of Turkey and also the home of the Patriarchy of the Eastern Orthodox Church. Much is said about the city and its importance in the modern world, and the fact that it is the only city to bridge two continents is often mentioned.

It is a noisy, polluted, busy and frustrating city. It is also beautiful, rich, diverse and strangely attractive for somewhere that has had so much bad publicity for centuries. As the melting pot of Turkey, attracting residents from all over the country who are either escaping poverty and violence or seeking an education, career and a cosmopolitan life the equal of few international cities, Istanbul is a city that embraces a wealth of cultures, languages, religions and lifestyles from Europe to the Middle East.

The Aegean Coast

Inland from the Aegean coast is a rich fertile agricultural region, stretching eastwards for many hundreds of kilometres. It often appears as a bit of a blank spot for package tourists, but it has a special place in history and an important part in Turkey's recent history and economic well-being.

Ancient Troy, biblical Nicaea, the first Ottoman capital at Bursa and Pergamum all sit in this region. As do towns less well-known but equally important – Kütahya (known for its tiles), Afyon (translates as opium) and Eskişehir (known for its meerschaum).

The orchards of the region produce fruit juice drunk in Europe and the olive groves produce some vintage oil, though tariffs prevent it reaching

Europe as well. The bright yellow fields of sunflowers add colour in the summer and supply the seeds endlessly chewed by Turkish men in the cafés.

The rich agricultural land meant it was settled and farmed for centuries and there are plenty of architectural gems, from many creeds and rulers left to demonstrate its history. In 1923 the Greeks also decided they wanted it for themselves and invaded. They moved far inland and almost reached Ankara before being driven back to the coast.

The final battle of the war left the old city of Smyrna in flames, with each side blaming the other for its destruction. Modern Izmir is built on the ruins of its predecessor and whilst it is a large and bustling metropolitan city and centre of trade, it has little of the character of Istanbul.

Mass tourism first arrived in Turkey on the Aegean coast and long stretches have been buried under concrete. There are, however, unspoilt and quiet corners to be found as the majority of package tours now head south of Izmir where the weather is warmer and the season is longer.

South of Izmir the concentration of ancient ruins manages to intensify. There are some seriously famous ruins here – Ephesus, Aphrodisias, the house of Mary (the mother of Jesus) and the tomb of St John to name but a few. The stunning travertine pools at Pamukkale, the crusader castle at Bodrum and Temple of Apollo at Didyma are also places well worth travelling to. The places you pass getting there, though, will be so distracting you could well get sidetracked along the way.

The Mediterranean Coast

The Aegean changes into the Mediterranean at Marmaris, one of the most developed tourist areas. Resort hotels, aquaparks, golf courses, marinas and holiday villages line the water and offer the chance to enjoy a beach holiday from April to October.

Like the Aegean coast, the Mediterranean is not totally spoilt and there are quiet beaches and small villages still to be found if you look hard enough.

Ancient sites still pop up round every corner and even in the sea cliffs, where tombs were carved by the Lycians. The beach at Dalyan has something special about it as it is one of the last breeding grounds of loggerhead turtles.

St Nicholas hails from the village of Demre and the fourth century priest, known as Noel Baba in Turkey, is believed to be the source of the story of Santa Claus and his benevolent gifts.

Mount Olympos and the flames of the Chimaera are not far from the ancient port of Antalya and the mausoleum of Priape is close by, and still proud, too. At certain times of year it is possible to ski in the Taurus mountains behind Antalya and swim in the sea the same day.

Past Alanya with its striking fort and 11th century walls and mostly German tourists, the package tours have faded from memory and the towns become more workmanlike with fewer sites and facilities to attract tourists.

Ferries to northern Cyprus run from Taşucu and the tomb of St Thekla (St Paul's first convert) is near Silifke. Tarsus is east of the new port city of Mersin and is supposedly where Cleopatra met Anthony, as well being the birthplace of St Paul.

The trading city of Adana has grown fast since Turkey came into being and is the last place of note before the coast turns south to Iskendurun (named after Alexander the Great) and home to one of the most popular food dishes in Turkey (Iskender kebab).

Iskendurun was occupied by the British and French after the First World War and then became part of Syria. It is also the end of the oil pipeline from northern Iraq and an unremarkable place.

The last town before Syria is Antakya and this Arabic town has lots of history, but little to show for it as it is frequently hit by earthquakes. Everyone who has figured in the history of the region seems to have fought over the strategically important town which even gained independence for a short while in 1938–39, as the Republic of Hatay (including Iskendurun), until Atatürk reclaimed it for Turkey.

What there is to see is the archaeology museum which contains some extensive and impressive Roman mosaics as well as some older artefacts from the days when Antakya was better known as Antioch and home to the fast growing Christian church. On the edge of town is the well preserved cave church of St John that is a popular place of pilgrimage.

Southwards is Syria, some 36 miles away.

The Black Sea Coast

The coastline where Jason and the Argonauts searched for the Golden Fleece is very different from that of the Aegean and Mediterranean. It is cooler, wetter and much greener than its counterparts and has nowhere near the number of obvious ancient ruins.

What it does offer is the chance to enjoy a much more relaxed lifestyle and the opportunity to see a traditional and little-changed Turkish way of life.

The towns are nothing special, many having been destroyed by earthquakes or by invaders. The weather does not help much either and there are many Ottoman era wooden houses dotted around the area that are falling into disrepair.

Though the ancient monuments are not so common or so famous, there is stunning scenery, excellent food, quiet beaches and a few monuments that are worth making a special trip to visit.

Amasra is a five hour drive north of Ankara and is famous for its seafood. Sitting on the terrace of a fish restaurant, built over the rocky shore of the Black Sea and watching the fishermen land the catch that will be on your plate in a few minutes is an experience not to be missed.

The fortified town of Sinop further east was involved in the build-up to the Crimean War, when it was attacked by the Russians. The attack led to the Ottoman Sultan joining with Britain to fight back against Russia.

Trabzon, formerly known as Trebizond, featured as a stopping-off point for many adventurers on their way east to join the Great Game in Central Asia.

It is now a port city bringing in goods from Istanbul for the eastern Black Sea region, as well as sending out the produce of the region.

Trabzon is home to the Aya Sofia Church, originally built in the 13th century. It is now a museum but is well worth visiting for the mosaics and iconographic paintings.

Almost 30 miles south of Trabzon is another religious site, the monastery at Sumela. Founded over 1,600 years ago, the current building is a relatively young 650 years old. Only the fit and healthy can reach the dizzying heights as the building clings to the rock face hundreds of metres above the valley floor.

Further along the coast is Rize, famous for the tea that carries its name. Along with tea, the Black Sea coast produces cherries, tobacco and especially hazelnuts in abundance, so much so that one town is named hazelnut (Fındıklı).

The region was home to Greek and Armenian communities in the days of the Ottoman Empire and there are still communities of Caucasian descent living on the eastern Black Sea Coast. The Laz and Hemşin ethnic groups are concentrated in the area east of Trabzon past Rize and in the town of Fındıklı you are as likely to hear Lazçe as Turkish spoken. The Hemşin live inland in the Kaçkar mountains around Çamlıhemşin and Ayder.

Central Anatolia

You would not know to look at it, but Central Anatolia is the breadbasket of Turkey. In summer it is hot, dry, brown and dusty. In winter it can be bitterly cold with snow on the ground for weeks and months on end in a bad winter.

Only for a few short weeks in spring do the hills go green and the flowers bloom, just in time for the tortoises to come out of hibernation along with the human residents.

Ankara was chosen as the modern capital partly because of where it is, in the middle of nowhere, and partly as a symbolic break with the old Ottoman Empire. Only 20,000 people lived in Ankara when Atatürk chose it as the political home of the new country he was trying to create and the British Ambassador of the time refused to move there as he considered it not of an acceptable standard for someone of his station to live in.

Despite its remoteness, the invading Greek army almost made it to Ankara in 1922, before the Turkish army stalled the advance and finally pushed them back to the Aegean.

Ankara's old town is small, though relaxed and picturesque, with few of the hassles prevalent in other historic cities of Turkey. The historically important temple of Augustus and Rome, which sits on a site important to various religions for millennia, is hidden alongside the Hacı Bayram Mosque, named after the founder of the famous Dervish sect.

There are other ancient remains around Ankara, but whilst they are often nothing special compared with other places in Turkey, their incongruous positions in modern streets and the carelessness with which the locals sit on them or ignore them, rather than charge you to look at them is refreshing.

Modern Ankara is home to the government, government agencies, the military, diplomats, universities and civil servants, making it a staunchly middle class city. The suburbs and surrounding villages, though, are often supporters of the new Islamist parties and the 1997 post-modern coup was played out in the Sincan suburb when the tanks rumbled past the mayor's offices.

In memory of the secularist founder of Turkey and modern Ankara is the massive mausoleum built to hold Atatürk's coffin, which is visible from much of the city. Designed in the style of the great classical temples, it is a blend of the cultures and landscape of Anatolia and was built to last as long.

To the west of Ankara, near the Sakarya River, where the Greek advance was halted, is Gordion. Alexander the Great cut The Knot here with a sword, in his frustration at being unable to untie it. Though not particularly spectacular, the site makes a pleasant trip from Ankara and there are scores of tumuli dotted around the area. One undisturbed royal tomb has been excavated and a passageway allows entry into the burial chamber at its heart.

Almost 160 miles due south of Ankara is the deeply religious city of Konya, which also sits in isolated splendour on the Anatolian plateau. Driving between the two cities, on the straight Roman roads, can be a tedious journey and certainly impresses on the traveller the emptiness and size of the region.

Full of mosques and *caravanserais*, Konya is a large city growing rich and more populous on the crops the never ending plateau sends to its markets. The old heart of the city has been settled since the bronze age and nearby Çatalhöyük lays claim to be the oldest human settlement yet discovered.

Konya is also home to the Whirling Dervishes following their expulsion from Ankara by Atatürk for being too political. Their annual festival is a highlight of the tourist calendar and the city becomes very busy at this time.

The other jewel in the Anatolian crown is Cappadocia, another historically important area that was home to the Hittites as well as early Christian communities. As waves of invading armies poured off the steppe of Central Asia, the inhabitants of the area moved underground, carving homes and cities in the soft mud left by the three local volcanoes. As well as underground cities there are homes in the conical towers of volcanic ash left when the surrounding detritus was washed and worn away. With a magical quality to the landscape and the aesthetic beauty of the underground cities and painted churches, a growing number of foreigners are running tourist businesses, alongside the locals, to tap into the special interest tour market that sits alongside the more budget conscious backpacker trail.

Apart from tourism, carpets are big business in Anatolia and the city of Kayseri has a name for offering some of the finest carpets around, though the merchants also have a reputation for driving a hard bargain.

Northern Anatolia is not as well travelled as the south, but the old Ottoman houses of Safranbolu and the rock-hewn Pontic tombs of Amasya are a draw for some, as are the ruins of the Hittite city at Hattuşaş. Safranbolu is also famous for the saffron produced in the area, after which the town is named.

Eastern Anatolia and the South East

Eastern Anatolia is Turkey in all its Central Asian glory. There are few concessions to western sensibilities and all the opportunities to experience the culture a visitor could want. The cities are ancient and full of history and reflect the numerous cultures that have invaded, ruled and inhabited Anatolia. It is easy to forget that approximately half of Turkey spreads further east from where the Mediterranean coast turns southwards.

Arabs, Russians, Armenians and Georgians, as well as the older cultures of the Romans, Persians and Hittites, have all left their mark on the remote and mountainous region.

Nemrut Dağ is one of the most striking ancient sites, where a ruler with a major sense of his own importance erected massive statues and had himself buried under an artificial 150 foot peak on the mountaintop.

Agri Dağ, better known as Mount Ararat outside of Turkey, is the legendary resting place of Noah and his ark. No ark has ever been found, but many people have come to look for it. Today it is climbers who mostly come, to scale its snow covered peak.

It is not only historical rulers and residents who have made an impact on the region. To help with the economic development of the region the government has built a huge hydroelectric power station and complex system of dams that stores and utilises water from the Euphrates and Tigris rivers. The cheap electricity and plentiful irrigation water has produced a boom economy and the government hopes to head off some of the issues fuelling the Kurdish uprising by raising the economic wealth of the area.

Lake Van was formed by nature, when a stream of lava from a now extinct volcano blocked a valley and cut off the river. With no outflow the lake level is maintained by evaporation and, much like the Dead Sea, this has resulted in a high mineral content. The lake is very alkaline and makes swimming with any skin wound a painful experience.

Travelling is not so easy in eastern Anatolia, but the rewards are great. Georgian and Armenian churches remain around Kars and Artvin. In Divriği UNESCO has designated the Selçuk mosques and other buildings as world heritage sites. At Doğubeyazit the Ishak Paşa Sarayı gives splendid views from is terraces and you can get a feel for the power of the Kurdish leader who built the complex over 300 years ago.

At the southern gateway to eastern Anatolia is Gaziantep, or Antep as it was known until given the honorific Gazi (war hero) for its defence against an invading French army in 1920. Having stayed clear of much of the violence associated with the Kurdish uprising, Gaziantep has grown rich and economically strong, but despite its long history there is only a small old quarter.

Şanlıurfa, on the other hand, has plenty of history to offer. Reputedly the birthplace of Abraham, there is also a massive medieval fortress and bazaar with *bedestans*, *çarşi* and *caravanserais* left over from when this was an important stopover on the trade routes. Nearby is the town of Harran, mentioned in Genesis, that is famous for its beehive-shaped houses. The Syrian Orthodox Church came into being here after a theological dispute over doctrine between the local bishop and the Patriarch in Constantinople.

In the heart of Kurdish territory is Mardin, a delightful town of stone-built houses and wonderful old religious buildings in the crowded narrow streets of the bazaar. The former seat of the Syrian Orthodox Church is a few miles out of town and sits on a site once used as a temple to worship the sun. Despite many incarnations, it is claimed that part of the original temple and sacrificial altar still remains in the depths of the existing monastery.

The most eastern Turkish city is Van, near Iran. Once capital city of the Urartians and later home to the Armenians, Van has been governed by many invaders and fought over by as many more. During the First World War the Armenians, who had previously been loyal to the Sultan in Constantinople, joined with the Russians and fought against Kurdish and Turkish forces. The Armenians had been hoping to form an independent Armenia, but the Russians took control of Van in 1915 and held it until the Armistice of 1917. Old Van was destroyed in the vicious fighting and the new city was built a few miles away after the war by the Turks. Despite the end of the First World War, fighting continued as Armenia declared independence in a small area of the land it claimed. During the next five years almost a million Armenians died, as well as hundreds of thousands of Kurds and Turks. The argument still continues as to whether it was genocide or a natural consequence of war.

Diyarbakir, the capital of the Kurdish region has seen its population swell to over two million since the Kurdish uprising began in the 1980s. Another ancient city, the great black basalt walls that circle the old quarter add to a feeling of age. The sense of living on the edge adds to the excitement (or fear) of being in a city at the heart of the Kurdish fight for independence. The old city is a maze of narrow alleyways and has an Arabic feel, which completes the transition from Turkey's European lands in Thrace.

2
Getting There

Turkey is a large country, sharing land borders with seven countries (Greece, Bulgaria, Georgia, Armenia, Iran, Iraq, Syria), as well as having an extensive coastline offering ferry links to Cyprus, Italy and Russia and sailing routes to Europe, the Middle East and North Africa. There are numerous ways to enter and leave the country, which provide plenty of choice for residents and tourists alike.

FLYING

In recent years the Turkish government has rebuilt, extended or otherwise improved many airports around the country, and the flying experience is much the better for it. The main international arrival point is Istanbul's Atatürk Airport (www.ataturkairport.com), which is a modern and spacious building and a symbol of the rapidly modernising economy as well as Istanbul's position as economic capital of Turkey. Ankara airport has similarly been upgraded to reflect its status as point of entry to the political capital of the country.

The national airline of Turkey is Turkish Airlines (Türk Hava Yolları – THY), but with the boom in tourism there are plenty of other options when travelling to the country. Numerous national airlines operate scheduled flights to Istanbul's Atatürk Airport, and to a lesser extent, Esenboğa Airport in Ankara and Adnan Menderes Airport in Izmir.

In addition, holiday companies operate hundreds of charter flights to a number of airports on the Aegean and Mediterranean coasts. These primarily operate during the tourist season that runs from approximately late April to late October.

Flight information, including arrivals and departure details, for all of Turkey's domestic and international airports can be found on the website of the General Directorate of State Airports Authority (Devlet Hava Meydanları İşletmesi – www.dhmi.gov.tr).

Of the national airlines offering flights to Turkey, not all are direct and some operate code share agreements with other airlines. Most national airlines flying out of Turkey will offer connecting flights from their home country to many other parts of the world, often at a lower price than if you choose a direct flight from Turkey to your final destination. There may also be the opportunity to enjoy a stopover at little or no additional cost. A few of the major operators flying to Turkey are listed in Appendix A.

Turkish Airlines (Türk Hava Yolları) fly to many international destinations and operate code share agreements with a number of airlines to facilitate connecting flights from airports in Europe and the Middle East to many places beyond.

Rather than booking flights direct with airlines, or using a high street travel agent, many passengers are now using online booking agents to source the best price for tickets. The online agents have the advantage that they check many airlines, routes and schedules simultaneously and allow you to make an informed choice as to which suits your needs best.

FERRIES AND SAILING

With such a long coastline that faces onto three seas (Aegean, Mediterranean and Black), arriving by boat is a great way to enter the country.

The Greek islands lie so close to Turkey that many of them can be seen with the naked eye while lying on a beach, while a pair of binoculars will let you see people walking around. Though the Greek islands are definitely the closest points from which to enter Turkey by sea, Cyprus, Italy and Ukraine are also options.

The Greek island ferries are aimed at day trippers, but combined with an island hopping holiday they make a great way to arrive in and depart from Turkey.

The routes from the Ukraine, Northern Cyprus and Italy offer the additional option of taking your car, and for the Italian and Ukrainian routes the journey times are so long it is almost like being on a cruise.

The main routes are listed in Appendix A, along with websites for the operators where appropriate. Routes to and from Greece are usually advertised locally in the operator's office or through agents, with the schedules depending on current demand. Not all the routes will operate during the winter.

OVERLAND

Driving

In the days of the hippie trail from Europe to Afghanistan and India, Turkey saw a lot of people in transit in their VW campervans, buses and cars. Nowadays few people drive across the country *en route* to anywhere else. However, there is a significant number of foreigners who live in the country who drive back and forth from Europe. These foreign residents are far outnumbered, though, by the Turks who make the trip home from Germany where they work.

The most popular and by far the cheapest route was traditionally through Yugoslavia and then Bulgaria. The Balkan wars put a stop to that route for a while and though the alternative through Hungary to Romania and then Bulgaria took over, it became increasingly problematic due to crime. Despite peace returning to the Balkans, the overland route is still complicated by the high crime rate in the southern countries and long delays at the Bulgarian border.

To avoid the Balkans the other obvious route is to drive down through Italy and either take a boat to Greece and then drive through Thrace to enter Turkey at Edirne, or take a ferry all the way from Italy to Turkey.

If you do not want to drive, there are also bus services direct to Turkey from Austria and Germany, as well as indirect services requiring a stopover in Greece at either Athens or Thessaloniki.

Coming from the other direction, it is possible to cross into Turkey from Georgia, Iraq, Armenia, Iran and Syria, though the crossing from Iraq will be problematic due to frequent border closures and ongoing fighting between the Turkish army and the PKK. That's even assuming you want to be in Iraq in the first place.

Train

For those with time to spare and a propensity to travel in a more laid back way, taking the train is always an option.

There are two ways to travel by train, either using a standard point-to-point ticket, or by using a railpass that allows you to break your journey where you want and take your time.

The InterRail (www.interrail.com) ticket is the best known rail pass in Europe and offers travel in 30 participating countries. Alternatively, standard international train tickets can be bought from a variety of travel agents and websites, or at main rail stations in most countries.

From Europe the route options are similar to when driving and there are daily trains from Greece, Hungary, Romania, Serbia and Bulgaria to Istanbul. From Greece there are direct trains from Thessaloniki, crossing the border at Edirne and terminating in Istanbul.

Starting at Belgrade another route passes through Sofia on its way to Istanbul. For a longer trip, there is the two day journey from Budapest that goes via Bucharest and Sofia.

From the east there are train services linking Turkey with Syria and Iran. Trains run from Tehran, via Tabriz, to Tatvan, with a ferry connecting to Van and onward trains to Ankara. Tickets and timetables can be found on the Iranian train operators website (www.rajatrains.com/indexe.asp).

From Syria the trains leave from Aleppo and run through Adana and on to

Konya. Syrian Railways has a website (www.cfssyria.org), but your Arabic will need to be good as there is no English section.

Printed European and world train timetables are available from Thomas Cook Publishing (www.thomascookpublishing.com), which helps with planning and booking long distance trips.

Tickets in Asia are relatively cheap compared to Europe, which makes European rail passes well worth their initial investment as they can significantly reduce the overall cost of travel in Europe when covering long distances.

SHIPPING OF PERSONAL BELONGINGS

Apart from getting yourself to Turkey you will probably want to take at least some, if not all, of your personal belongings with you. How you get them there will depend a lot on how much you want to take with you.

If you travel light and only want to take a few small items, you may well be able to carry everything with you when you travel. On the other hand, if you decide to take enough to fill a house you will have to arrange a removal company to take everything for you.

Deciding what you want to take is a very personal decision. Some expatriates take all their worldly possessions every time they move, no matter where they go. Others sell almost everything they own and travel with nothing but one suitcase, then buy everything new once they arrive at the next destination.

A lot will depend on what it is that makes you feel at home in the place where you live. For some people a few photos of friends and family scattered around will suffice. Other people find that they want, or need, to have familiar furniture, bed linen, books and other items around them.

When planning your move it is worth considering what it is that makes the place you live into a home and whether that can be bought in Turkey or whether you will need to take it with you. You will also need to consider how many items of sentimental value you want to take with you, and what you are happy to leave in storage while you are living abroad.

If you have children then you will need to consider what will help them make as smooth a transition as possible. Favourite toys, pictures, DVDs and other items can help them settle in their new home and provide a sense of security when they find themselves in a new culture far away from the only home they have previously known.

A further consideration is the requirement for a customs bond to be lodged with a bank for personal items temporarily imported into Turkey. The cost of this may make transporting a large amount of items prohibitive and actually make it cheaper to sell up and buy new once you arrive.

Electrical items may also not work, or require an adaptor, depending on where you move from. Televisions and DVDs in Turkey operate on the PAL system, so American, Canadian and French televisions and DVD players will not work at all, even allowing for voltage adaptors that allow them to operate on the 230V electricity supply of Turkey.

Choosing how you will transport your belongings will also depend on how you travel there. If you are driving you may well find that you can fit everything you want into your own car. When flying it may not be possible to carry everything you want to take.

There are a variety of ways to transport your personal effects to Turkey, including:

- international postal service;
- excess baggage when flying;
- excess baggage via an air courier based in an airport departure terminal;
- air cargo using an international freight forwarding agency;
- surface cargo using an international freight forwarding agency;
- international removal company.

The international postal service will be useful for relatively small packages that you do not need immediately. Surface mail can be very slow and take many months to arrive in Turkey from North America.

Excess baggage services are quick and your luggage will arrive on the same flight for an accompanied service and only a few days later for an unaccompanied service. This service is great for suitcase-sized bags, but can be expensive as airlines will often charge a percentage of the first class airfare for excess baggage.

Air cargo, sent using a freight forwarder is cheaper than an excess baggage service and bulkier items can be sent this way, but air cargo is also charged on a per kilo basis and can become expensive. Surface cargo will often be cheaper than air cargo and will be charged by volume, but this will be much slower and may take weeks to arrive, even from Europe.

The alternative to arranging the shipping of a large amount of your personal belongings yourself is to use an international removal company to do all the work on your behalf. This can certainly be easier and less stressful as an expert will take care of all the arrangements for you, leaving you to concentrate on moving yourself to the new country and getting settled without having to worry about all the paperwork.

Further information and resources on relocating are included in Appendix A.

SHIPPING OF PETS

When planning the travel arrangements for your pet you have two options: you can either make all the arrangements yourself, or use a specialist pet transport company to secure the paperwork, complete the vaccination programme and arrange the flights. Whichever option you choose, you must still arrive in Turkey at the same time as your pet.

Making all the arrangements yourself is usually straightforward, but will require careful planning to ensure all the paperwork is completed in sequence and within the right timescale.

The general requirements for taking a cat or dog into Turkey are listed below, but you should always check the current requirements with your local Turkish Embassy or Consulate when making your travel plans.

- The animal must be micro-chipped with an international standard chip meeting ISO standards.

- Dogs need to have the following vaccinations: Distemper, Hepatitis, Parvovirus, Leptospirosis, (DHLPP).

- Cats need to have the following vaccinations: Feline Viral Rhinotracheitis, Calicivirus, Panleukopenia (FVRCP).

- Cats and dogs must have had a recent rabies vaccination (not longer than 12 months and not less than four weeks before arrival in Turkey).

- A valid import permit from the Turkish Embassy or Consulate.

- A valid international health certificate issued not more than ten days before departure and endorsed by the local Department of Agriculture (or equivalent) or a designated person.

At the point of arrival you will need:

- the pet owner's passport;

- the original rabies certificate;

- the original international health certificate;

- the original import permit.

Contact your preferred airline prior to booking your tickets to ensure that the airline accepts pets and that there is space on the specific flight for your animal. Some airlines limit the number of live animals and at peak times these spaces fill up quickly.

Other questions to ask include:

- Does the airline have any special pet health and immunisation requirements over and above the requirements on the destination country?

- Is a specific type of carrier required?

Direct flights are preferable as take off and landing can be especially stressful for your pet and transfers increase the handling of the pet carrier which can also be stressful. Tranquillisers are not recommended as they add to the dehydration effects of the flight and can cause your pet additional distress.

When travelling in the summer or winter months where there are extreme highs or lows in temperature, try to choose a flight that will avoid the worst of the temperature extremes during loading and unloading of the aircraft.

Always attach a number of labels to the pet carrier with your contact details and the contact details of someone at the final destination. Where possible include your mobile phone number if it will still work at your destination.

Introduce your pet to the carrier well before the flight so they can become accustomed to its smell and interior, this will further reduce stress during the flight.

Feeding is not recommended before or during the flight as it increases the likelihood of vomiting. A drip water bottle is the preferred method of ensuring an adequate supply of drinking water during the flight and allows fresh water to be supplied at stopovers without opening the carrier.

Finally, when boarding the flight, notify the aircrew that your pet is travelling in the cargo hold and ask them to check it is aboard.

TRAVELLING WITH CHILDREN

It goes without saying that travel is an integral part of expatriate living. Without travelling at least once it would be impossible to become an expatriate. When you're single, or one of a couple, the travel part can be fun, exciting, romantic and adventurous, an escape from normality. As the saying goes, 'A change is a good as a rest'.

But add a couple of kids, especially a baby, and the likelihood of being able to rest diminishes sharply and the fun, excitement and adventure become more of a logistical nightmare.

Planes, airports and travel *can* be exciting for children, there is so much going on and so much to see. But a few hours spent inside a metal tube, confined to a small area of seating, with nothing to look at but clouds, or even worse a blank night sky, and the time can begin to drag terribly.

Stopovers *en route* can be a good way to break up a particularly long journey, but beware, some airports are definitely not child friendly.

During the flight your child's boredom will be the biggest problem you'll be up against. On a 14 hour flight, what are you to do with the kids? Apart from the actual travelling time there is the disruption to the child's routine, with meals and drinks coming when the airline decides. Throw in time differences, disrupted sleep patterns and jet-lag and you find yourself with a fractious child and grumpy neighbours on the plane.

However, with careful planning, good research and a child-friendly airline, you can mitigate many of the problems and hopefully reduce the potential stress and upset.

Get in touch with the information desk of your potential carrier and ask them what services they provide for children. Sometimes there are special children's services and facilities available at no extra cost, (drawing kits, children's movie/cartoon channel, personal video games, etc.), there may even be a special play area at the airport if it is the airline's home base. Often these services are not heavily promoted, you just have to ask for them to get them. Knowing what services an airline offers can help you choose the best one for your circumstances.

Most airports have websites now and will list the services they offer, this can be helpful when deciding where to have a stopover or change flights *en route* to Turkey.

- Airports Worldwide is developing reviews of many airports, including some obscure little ones, as well as links to their websites: www.airports-worldwide.com.

- Skytrax lists passenger reviews of airlines and airports websites, though most are from business travellers: www.airlinequality.com.

Below are some tips to help smooth the journey, for you, your children and other passengers:

- When travelling east to west on a long-haul flight, try to keep your kids up late enough to take a late evening flight; hopefully they will then fall asleep for much of the flight as soon as it takes off. This will give you and your fellow travellers, as well as the children themselves a few hours' rest so that when they do wake up they should be refreshed and not too grumpy, bored or fidgety. You will also be likely to arrive at your destination airport early in the morning, have time and daylight to reach your new accommodation and get settled in. The children will then have a good stretch of daylight to see their new home and be ready for bed again at roughly the right time of day, so helping them get over their jet-lag.

- When you are travelling east to west on a long-haul flight and cannot keep your kids up late enough to take a late evening flight, try to leave home early in the morning. That way you will arrive at your destination airport in the evening and you can go straight to a hotel, sleep and hope to avoid the worst of the jet lag.

- Travelling west to east often seems to cause the worst jet-lag for many people. With long-haul trips in this direction, time-zone changes speed the clock forward, making journeys appear days long. Try to time your arrival for late afternoon or dusk, so your body clock experiences the end of the day, then you will be able to think about sleeping and minimize the effects of the jet-lag.

- Choose a child-friendly airline by checking airline websites, traveller review sites and phoning airlines directly for information.

- Contact the airline in advance to book a child seat (like a car safety seat) for smaller children. This raises them up closer to your level and eases interaction during the flight. A child seat holds the child more securely than a simple lap strap and when they sleep it leaves you free to relax without having a baby on your knee.

- Use backpacks to carry your luggage instead of suitcases and standard carry-on bags. Hands-free backpacks leave you better able to pick up loose belongings, carry drinks and snacks and keep hold of your child in the busy crowds at airports and on dangerous tarmac areas when boarding the plane.

- Make the trip fun and involve your child by getting them to help you to pack a small bag that they will be able to carry themselves and which will include their favourite books and quiet toys.

- Bring some new storybooks, colouring books and crayons as a surprise for your child. Remember to make sure the books are small enough to fit on airline sized tables and be manageable in the confined spaces of an aeroplane.

- Bring along snacks of cheese, fruit and other favourite finger foods and keep them within easy reach in your carry on bag. Avoid packing chocolate and other sugary foods, as well as those that make too much mess. Pack small drink cartons, with straws, as airline travel can be very dehydrating and the sucking action can help relieve ear pressure during take off and landing. Drinks with a high sugar content should be avoided as they can add to the dehydrating effects of air travel. Also pack wet wipes, even if your child is out of nappies, to clean sticky fingers after snacks.

- On very long journeys consider a stopover half-way through the journey. Singapore is a great place to stop on the way from Australia or New Zealand, as is London on the way from America or Canada.

CULTURE SHOCK

Though culture shock will not generally happen until after you arrive, it is still an integral part of the moving experience. Culture shock is something you will undoubtedly experience every time you move, to a greater or lesser extent.

Culture shock can even happen when you move within a country. If you move from rural Cornwall to inner city London you are going to suffer as much, if not more, as if you move from New York to Istanbul.

Culture shock is a physical as well as an emotional experience and can be defined as the result of stress due to unfamiliar surroundings. Culture shock can definitely be as much due to physical impacts as emotional ones. Climate, clothing, altitude, food and personal comfort are as much components of culture shock as the language, traditions, attitudes and religion that make up the cultural component of a country.

Culture shock can sometimes be seen as something to be overcome in a battle of wills, but this attitude can often make the problem worse. The alternative of protecting yourself from the local way of life and trying to carry on as is if you had never left home can often make the problem worse too. Trying to change the way things are done in Turkey to make it more like what you are used to is only going to make you frustrated. Learning to understand why, or how, a task is accomplished the way it is, can often be a more successful way to diffuse your frustrations than trying to change the method.

Learn the Language

Learning Turkish can save you a lot of problems too. By learning the language you can begin to understand your unfamiliar surroundings and realise that the person who you think is trying to stop you taking a short cut is actually trying to tell you that the road is blocked along the way, or that he will give a you lift in his car if you wait for a few minutes.

At the very least, being able to buy a drink in a restaurant and to recognise some of the foods listed on the menu will help you relax and begin to feel as though you are not totally out of your comfort zone.

Understand the Country

One way to reduce the impact of your culture shock is to learn as much about Turkey as possible before you relocate. By reading books, visiting travel agents, watching movies, surfing the internet and listening to the major news programmes you will be able to learn something of what makes the country tick and prepare yourself for some of the major differences you will meet. Chat groups and expatriate websites where you can read about the country and ask questions of people already there can also be a good way of getting to know people and making friends, so there may even be a welcoming face when you arrive.

If you can generate some enthusiasm and a sense of excitement about your move, and have a list of places to visit and things you want to see, then you are much more likely to enjoy the country once you get there.

Coping with Culture Shock

You should always remember though, that no matter how much preparing you do, you will still suffer culture shock. It may be mild, but it will still happen.

The first few days and weeks after arrival are often a honeymoon period when everything is new and exciting. Every trip outside will be a time of discovery and will be like being on holiday.

For some people this sense of excitement and discovery hardly falls off, but for most people the frustrations of the differences and things they do not understand begin to knock the edge off the excitement.

When it takes weeks to get a telephone and internet connection sorted out, or get a new fridge delivered, life takes on a less rosy tint. Working past any frustration and anger that develops is the next stage of culture shock. For some it will take effort and a will to succeed and you need to remember that no one is going to do it for you.

These few weeks can be a make or break time as to whether you will ever settle in Turkey. If you give up and decide it's too hard to learn the language, understand the Turkish culture and way of doing things, or there is no point in trying to make a home for yourself, you are likely to be stuck with the frustration and anger. When this happens you can get to the point where you spend most of your time wishing you could leave the country.

However, if you keep working at getting used to the way of life, then one day you will discover that you are enjoying yourself. When you can understand the shopkeeper, the taxi driver knows where you want to go and the waiter recognises you when go to your favourite restaurant, all the effort will seem worthwhile.

When you begin to relax into the culture of Turkey you can really enjoy the country and all its pleasures. With friends, both Turkish and expatriate, you can experience the delights of a Turkish wedding, waterside barbecue parties and traditional Turkish hospitality, where customs and traditions you have read about in books are practised by real people.

Always remember though that culture shock can recur. Occasionally you can slip into times of frustration as the differentness of Turkey just becomes all too much to cope with. Some expatriates find their recurrences are seasonal, others at Christmas, Thanksgiving or birthdays, but for some it can be random and sudden.

Prepare yourself for recurring culture shock and have a plan to deal with it. Go out for dinner, cook yourself a favourite meal from home, or hang out with friends. But don't give up, because it's almost always easier to work through a recurrence than it is to get past the first experience of it.

Most of all, always try to remember why it is you wanted to move to Turkey in the first place and then make sure you make the most of that opportunity while you are there.

RELOCATING WITH CHILDREN

If you are moving to Turkey with children then it is worth considering the move from their point of view. Children will have different concerns and fears about such a move from those of any adult.

The way a child will react to such a move will vary, but you cannot assume they are necessarily happy about it, or unconcerned at the prospect of moving away from their friends and what is probably the only place they can remember living in.

There are several common and very real concerns that children have about an international move, many of which the parent will probably not have even considered. Such concerns include the belief that they:

- will live in the destination country for ever and never go back home;
- will be left behind when their parents make the move;
- will be abandoned abroad;
- will lose all their toys and personal possessions;
- will never see their friends and relatives again;
- will not have anywhere to live in the destination country;

- will not have a school to go to;
- will not have anyone to play with;
- will not be able to make friends in the destination country;
- will not find anything they like to eat;
- will not understand anything as no one will speak their language.

For a child the things that make the move exciting for the parents may have the opposite effect. Taking the time to identify something new and exciting the child can do at the destination, while acknowledging what they will leave behind, can help make the transition less frightening.

Despite the time and effort required to plan an international move, it is important to take the time to reassure your child and explain to them about the process of the move. Where applicable, tell them explicitly that personal belongings and pets will be going too and that whilst you are leaving one home and travelling to a new country, there will be somewhere to live and go to school in Turkey.

If possible, show them photos of your new home, their school, places they will find interesting and activities they will want to do. A pre-move visit can go a long way towards helping reassure children that the move can be positive.

Children can often get the wrong impression or gain a negative perception by mishearing something you say or by picking up on your stress. By involving the children in the process of moving you can reduce some of their concerns and by explaining to them what is going to happen, you can make the actual move less traumatic.

When their parents demonstrate a positive, but realistic, attitude towards a move, children can feel much more confident about the whole process too, but they will quickly pick up and adopt any negative attitude as well.

For children there will be three main stress points in the move:

- packing and sending your belongings;
- saying goodbye and leaving;
- arrival and settling in.

Each of these needs to be considered separately to help the child make as successful a move as possible.

Packing and Shipping

By taking as many of your child's personal belongings as possible you can help create a comfort zone in their new destination. This will help reassure them that their old life has not completely disappeared and that life will continue. When you are packing, always make it clear that the items are being taken with you, or being sent, to your new home,

Many international removal companies provide special services for families and children, in addition to the books that deal specifically with relocating children internationally. There are workbooks, storybooks and special shipping boxes for children's belongings. The boxes will help children identify their things and reassure them that they are on the lorry that takes everything away. They will also be able to find them quickly again at the destination when everything is being unloaded.

Saying Goodbye and Closure

Goodbyes are as important for children as they are for their parents. Children need to be reminded that friends and relatives will not forget them, and are waiting for them to return, either for visits or permanently. Making sure that your children know that you have invited people to visit you in Turkey can also help reassure them you are not saying goodbye for ever.

Though the actual goodbyes can be painful, they can leave children more comfortable in the longer term about living internationally.

Arriving and Settling In

Making your child feel comfortable and secure in Turkey will go a long way towards helping them settle in, make friends and enjoying living in the country. Give them time to build confidence and adjust to their new surroundings. Go for walks around the neighbourhood so they will not worry about getting lost if they go out alone, practise saying your new address together in Turkish and if they are old enough, buy them a mobile phone so they can always call you if they need to.

With such a big change children will often worry that other big changes will happen soon after. This can lead to disrupted sleep patterns and separation anxiety, so constant, but subtle, reassurance will be needed.

Moving from rural Wales to central London would be a culture shock for your child, and a move from Sussex to Ankara will be much the same.

By making your new home, and their bedroom in particular, a secure and comfortable base, your child will be able to explore their new surroundings and have somewhere to return to when they need time to consider and accept the new sights, sounds and smells they will find in Turkey.

Having a cosy and comfortable room will also make it easier for them to invite new friends to visit as well, which will further encourage the settling-in process.

3
Bureaucracy

Like any country, Turkey has its own bureaucratic system that a foreign resident must navigate on the way to gaining legal residence and setting up a home. Being outside the European Union means that Europeans do not have the right to move to Turkey as if they were moving from Britain to Spain. However, if you have a job, the finance to start a business, or enough money to fund your retirement, then moving to the country is not too difficult.

The first bureaucratic process to negotiate before moving to the country to live and work is the acquisition of a visa and a work permit. Once you arrive it is then necessary to secure a residence permit.

VISAS AND WORK PERMITS

Many nationalities require a visa to enter Turkey, even for a holiday. This requirement is based on reciprocity – if Turks need a visa to enter a country, then that country's citizens require a visa to enter Turkey.

Visa fees vary by nationality and it is always advisable to confirm the relevant fee in advance of submitting an application. Family members can submit applications simultaneously, but groups cannot. Tourist visas are often more expensive when bought in advance than when they are bought at the border (e.g. UK passport holders pay £50 in advance or £10 at point of entry).

Where required, a tourist visa is often obtainable at the port of entry, for cash. However, a work visa must be applied for in advance. A residence visa can be applied for prior to arrival in Turkey, or after arrival and expiration of the three month tourist visa. A residence visa application can take up to eight weeks to process.

A full list of countries requiring a visa is contained on the Turkish Embassy websites, of which there are a number in various countries (e.g. UK – www.turkishconsulate.org.uk; USA – www.turkishembassy.org).

Nationals of Australia, Canada, USA and the UK can all obtain a three month visa at the port of entry, as can EU nationals if they need one at all. For other nationalities the rules vary; for example, nationals of the Republic of South Africa need to apply in advance of travelling. Full details are available on the websites listed above.

Applications at an Embassy or Consulate must generally be made in person, though exemption can be granted from this restriction in extenuating circumstances. Credit cards, debit cards and personal cheques are not accepted for payment, but cash, postal orders and company cheques are.

Residence Visa

The process for obtaining a residence visa is straightforward, though somewhat regimented. If applying in the UK it is necessary to apply for a visa, in person, at the Turkish Consulate in London. An online appointment system operates via the embassy website (www.turkishconsulate.org.uk).

A completed application form needs to submitted at the time of your appointment and a form can be obtained from the website or by requesting one in writing from the Consulate as long as a stamped, self addressed envelope is provided with the request.

Your passport needs to be valid for at least six months from the date of entry to the country.

Work Visa

The application process for a work visa is similar to that for a residence visa, though an appointment needs to be made with the Labour Attaché at the Embassy or Consulate. A work visa application form is available on the Consulate website, or by requesting one in writing from the Consulate as long – once again – as a stamped, self addressed envelope is provided with the request.

It is also possible to obtain a work permit after entering the country providing you have a visitor's permit valid for at least six months. The process is similar to when applying from abroad but must be done through the Ministry of Labour and Social Security (www. yabancicalismaizni.gov.tr). Further details for employers on how to initiate the process of obtaining the work permit can also be obtained directly from the Ministry of Labour and Social Security, or via their website.

For a work visa your passport needs to be valid for at least a year after arrival and you will need to include the offer of employment along with your application.

Additional Documents

When applying for residence and work visas it is necessary to submit supporting documentation along with the visa application form. The necessary items are listed below.

Residence and Work Visas

- A passport-sized photo attached to the visa application form.
- Latest bank statement (original to be returned) and a photocopy. Bank statement must show the applicant's current financial standing.
- Relevant visa fee and administration fees.
- Self addressed envelope for return of passport.
- Letter specifying the reason for intended residence in Turkey.
- Details of pension or other regular income.
- Details of any assets in Turkey.
- Any other relevant supporting information.

Work Visas Only

You will need to submit proof of employment (e.g. offer letter from the prospective employer). Work visa applications will be referred back to Turkey where the employer will need to have submitted the relevant documentation to complete the visa authorisation process to the Labour and Social Security Ministry (Çalışma ve Sosyal Güvenlik Bakanlığı – www.calisma.gov.tr). Details of the documentation required from the employer can be found online on a website of the ministry specifically for foreign nationals applying for work permits: www.yabancicalismaizni.gov.tr.

Your prospective Turkish employer can find information on the process and application forms at www.csgb.gov.tr. When they have completed the relevant form the employer should return the paperwork to the Ministry of Labour and Social Security.

Applying for a Visa at a Consulate/Embassy Not in Your Home Country

You can apply for a visa in a country other than your own, but the application will be referred back to Turkey and will take considerably longer to process.

Residence Permit (*İkamet*)

With a residence and work visa in hand, you also need to register with the local police in Turkey, at the Foreigners' Office (Yabancılar Bürosu), within one month of arrival in order to obtain a residence permit. Residence permits are valid for limited periods and should be extended by application to the same police headquarters before the permit expires.

IMPORTING PERSONAL BELONGINGS

Household items may be taken into Turkey as temporarily imported bonded items for a period covered by a residence permit, where the residence permit is valid for at least one year. The items cannot be imported until the residence permit has been issued to the owner after their arrival in Turkey.

A full inventory of the items being shipped, which must be for personal use only and not brand new (so remove any packaging of items you buy for the move), is required by the shipping company to enable them to complete the import process. The personal use restriction is generally taken to mean that only one of any item of value (e.g. TV, radio, computer, etc.) per person is allowed. As all the items on the list must be re-exported, technically you cannot throw away any listed item, even if it breaks. Items can be removed from the list if you can face going through the system.

Most of the paperwork must be completed by the shipping company, or their agent, and a good one will provide advice on setting up the required bond. When organising your shipment always make sure that the agent you use on departure ensures the corresponding agent in Turkey is familiar with the process of importing the personal belongings of a foreigner. This should help smooth the process, which can be time-consuming and frustrating.

Further details can be obtained from the Office of the Finance and Customs Counsellor at any Turkish Embassy. Information on the process has previously been available on the website of the Turkish Customs Administration (T.C. Başbakanlık Gümrük Müsteşarlığı – www.gumruk. gov.tr), but at the time of writing was not.

Using a reputable and reliable removal company is well worth the cost, you certainly get what you pay for with removal companies. The International Federation of Removal Companies (Fédération Internationale des Déménageurs Internationaux, FIDI aisbl), 69 Rue Picard B-5, 1080 Brussels, Belgium; Tel +32 2 426 5160; Fax +32 2 426 5523; http://fidi. com and the European Relocation Association, P.O.Box 189, Diss IP22 1PE, England; Tel +44 870 072 6727; Fax +44 137 964 1940; www.eura-relocation.com both list their worldwide membership online, unless you can secure a good word of mouth recommendation for a specific removal company.

CURRENCY

After years of chronic and acute inflation, the Turkish Lira exchange rate was close to 2,000,000TL to the £1 (1,600,000TL to the US$). During one particularly bad month the currency slipped by almost 30%.

With the help of the IMF, Turkey instituted a wide-ranging economic restructuring programme and stabilised the exchange rate with a view to issuing a new currency with a more manageable rate.

On January 1st 2005 the New Turkish Lira (Yeni Turkçe Lira, YTL) was introduced to replace the existing Turkish Lira (TL), with 1YTL = 1,000,000TL. For one year the two sets of banknotes co-existed until January 1st 2006 when the TL was withdrawn. Old-style TL bank notes can be exchanged at Turkish Central Bank branches and T. C. Ziraat Bankasi branches in cities where there are no Central Bank offices.

The final component of the process will occur in 2009 when the Yeni will be removed from the currency and it will become TL once more over a further one year transition period. Again, there will be a ten year period to exchange outgoing notes and coins at the Central Bank or Ziraat Bankasi as appropriate.

1YTL is made up of 100 New Kurush (Yeni Kuruş) with 1, 5, 10, 20, 50 and 100YTL banknotes in circulation alongside coins of 1, 5, 10, 25 and 50 YK and 1YTL. During March 2008 the exchange rate for a variety of currencies was as below:

£1GB = 2.57YTL	1US$ = 1.29YTL
1AUD$ = 1.18YTL	1NZ$ = 1.02YTL
1CDN$ = 1.27YTL	1Euro = 2.03YTL

OWNING A VEHICLE

As a foreign resident it is possible to import a vehicle to the country, though it is easier to buy one after arrival. A residence permit is needed to import any vehicle, which must leave the country again when the owner permanently leaves Turkey. Alternatively, the vehicle can be sold to another foreigner staying in the country.

Importing a Vehicle

The process of importing a car is time-consuming and requires a hefty deposit (returnable when the car leaves Turkey or is sold on), as well as certain non-refundable fees to secure the Foreign Vehicle Temporary Carnet (Yabancı Taşitlar Geçici Giriş Karnesi), also known as a 'blue card' (which is neither blue nor a card).

Embassy personnel, former Turkish citizens, or people with dual Turkish citizenship cannot import or own a vehicle under the process described below.

To obtain a blue card, a residence permit, passport and driving licence (with photocopies), work permit (where appropriate), student certificate (where appropriate), vehicle ownership document and receipt/invoice (if available), confirmation of employment by employer, relevant deposit and a completed application form must be presented to the Turkey Touring and Automobile Association (Türkiye Turing ve Otomobil Kurumu). Along with the blue card, Turkish number plates will be issued that need to be attached to the vehicle until it is processed for re-export.

The value of the deposit is determined by the age and engine size of the vehicle and is set by the Turkey Touring and Automobile Association. The deposit can either be paid in cash, or be in the form of an acceptable bank guarantee letter. An up-to-date list of the relevant deposits can be found at www.turing.org.tr/html/teminatlistesieng.htm.

The validity of the blue card is determined by the duration of the residence/work permit, but can be extended once a residence/work permit is extended. There are penalties for failing to renew on time. All ownership documents and licences will need to be translated and notarised. The deposit cannot be returned until the vehicle is sold, re-exported or the blue card application process is reversed, the Turkish number plates returned and the original foreign number plates re-attached. There is then a limited time in which the vehicle must leave Turkey.

The fee for issuing the blue card, in addition to the deposit is 270YTL for one year, or 340YTL for two years. Renewal rates are 120YTL (six months), 205YTL (one year) and 320YTL (two years).

Vehicle Licensing

Every two years, vehicles over three years old are required to be tested for safety and the level of exhaust emissions. Until 2005 separate authorities carried out each test, but as part of the government's privatisation programme a contract was awarded to TÜV-TURK to build and operate approximately 200 testing stations throughout the country.

The safety test examines the basic structure of the vehicle, the brakes and accessories such as lights. The emissions test covers carbon monoxide levels and particulates in the exhaust output. Failure to produce a valid test certificate when requested by the relevant authorities is an offence and can result in a fine.

Vehicle Tax

All cars must be taxed individually and depending on the engine size and date of manufacture, the taxes for 2008 range from YTL12 to over YTL28,000. The tax is paid in two instalments in January and July every year.

Vehicle Category	Amount of Tax	
	Minimum tax (YTL)	Maximum tax (YTL)
Cars	105 (12–15 years old, 1300cc)	12,697 (1–3 years old, 4001+cc)
Motorbikes	12 (16+ years old, 100–250cc)	845 (1–3 years old, 1201+cc)
Minibus, bus, lorry, pick-ups	139	1,902
Yacht, boat or ship	280	6,400
Airplane and helicopter	3,384	28,218

Driving Licence

Either a full Turkish driving licence, or an International Driving Licence (also known as International Driver's Permit – IDP) in conjunction with a full driving licence from another country is required for driving in Turkey. International driving licences can be obtained from national motoring organisations (see Appendix A for organisations in various countries) in the country that issued your current licence, or from the country where you are currently resident, as well as from online companies which will issue a licence to accompany national licences from most countries in the world.

TRAFFIC REGULATIONS

Traffic drives on the right in Turkey, which has adopted the international convention on traffic signs. Road signs and speed limits are broadly similar to Europe, with the standard limits as listed below. Where a local variation is in place this will be signposted.

A minimum speed limit is in place on motorways (expressways) and speed limits are reduced by 10km/h if you are towing a trailer or caravan.

- Speed limit on urban roads – 50km/h.
- Speed limit on non-urban roads – 90km/h.
- Speed limit on motorways – 120km/h.

The wearing of seatbelts is mandatory in the front seats, but not in the rear seats and child seats are also optional. For use in the event of an accident, it is compulsory to carry a first aid kit, fire extinguisher and at least two red reflective warning triangles.

Despite your natural inclination to try and move a vehicle off the road and out of the way of other traffic if you have an accident, this must not be done until the police have arrived and given permission for the vehicle to be moved. Moving your vehicle before the police arrive is an offence in law and fines will be enforced. The traffic police (*trafik polisi*) can be contacted in urban areas on telephone number 154 and elsewhere the

Jandarma can be contacted on telephone number 156.

The fault of an accident can be split between two or more drivers, for example 60% the fault of driver A and 40% the fault of driver B. This is at the discretion of the attending police officer and the final decision will depend on the strength of your arguments during what will be a heated discussion between yourself, the police and the other driver.

All documentation (ownership, blue card, insurance, vehicle licence, vehicle tax) for the vehicle must be carried at all times, along with your national driving licence and international driver's permit, or a Turkish driving licence.

Drink driving limits are low with random breath tests common, and they are mandatory after an accident. If you are towing a caravan or trailer the alcohol limit is zero. Failure of a breath test will result in a fine and loss of your licence, with repeat offences punished more severely.

Road blocks are frequently set up and cars stopped randomly, or *en masse*. Tickets can be issued for no apparent reason with fines collected on the spot. Depending on the offence, fines will vary from YTL40 to YTL900, though discounts may be offered if you do not want a receipt.

PETS

Pets can be brought into Turkey as long as they travel with the owner. There is also a limit per person of the number of animals that can be imported such as one dog and one cat.

See pages 36–38 for specific information on importing pets.

For pets travelling from the USA the Turkish Embassy in Washington DC states that the following documents are necessary:

• a rabies vaccination certificate, which must be issued not later than fifteen days prior to entry;

• a 'United States Interstate and International Certificate of Health Examination for Small Animals' (also called Form 7001).

MARRIAGE

The process of arranging a wedding in Turkey is unlike in other countries. There are some strict and unusual restrictions laid down in law.

A Turkish national and non-Turkish national and two foreign nationals of different nationality can only get married in Turkey if they do so in a secular ceremony at a Turkish register office (*nüfus müdürlüğü*), under Turkish law. However, two foreign nationals of the same nationality also have the option of marrying in their own embassy under the rules of that country. If there is a requirement to marry under Turkish law, it is still possible to have a religious ceremony at the embassy church or elsewhere if desired.

All marriages under Turkish law require certain documents be presented before the marriage can take place, and these include a certificate of no impediment. For non-Turkish nationals this certificate can usually be obtained from your embassy.

To marry in Turkey you must be at least 18 years old and of sound mind and not suffer from certain illnesses (including epilepsy and hysteria!). An official health certificate is required to demonstrate this sound constitution. Bigamy and marriage between close relatives is illegal and divorced women must wait 300 days from the date of their divorce before they can remarry. Under Turkish law a divorce court can bar a 'guilty' spouse from remarrying for a certain period.

To marry under Turkish law it is necessary to provide the following documents to the registrar:

- a completed application form, or petition – *evlenme beyannamesi*;
- passport, identification card, birth certificate;
- health certificate;
- passport-style photo of each party;
- certificate of non-impediment signifying marriage status – i.e. single, divorced, widowed or widower.

A certificate of non-impediment can be obtained from your local registrar in your home country before you travel to Turkey, or if you reside in Turkey from your embassy. Such certificates may have a limited validity and a marriage will have to take place before it expires. For Britons the British Embassy will charge £59 for the certificate.

After a Turkish marriage it is advisable to register the marriage with your embassy for which you will need a copy of both the bride and groom's passport or ID card, the marriage certificate and a *formül B* obtained from the Turkish register office. The British Embassy charges £34 for the process.

DIVORCE

If your wedding took place in Turkey and you divorce outside the country, this does not necessarily mean your marriage is annulled in Turkey. A Turkish court would still consider you married and it is therefore advisable to ensure any such divorce is registered in Turkey to ensure you cannot be charged with bigamy if you ever visit the country again.

To divorce in Turkey you will need to be represented by a Turkish lawyer and possess a notarised copy of your passport or other ID, two passport photos; you'll also be required to pay a fee of approximately £20 (US$40). It is usual that the mother is given custody of any children, unless she is proven to be an unfit mother, which is not a straightforward process and requires a petition at court.

If you were not married in Turkey it is possible to gain a divorce in the country if both parties are currently living in Turkey, and agree to the process.

BIRTHS

Children born in Turkey are issued with a local birth certificate (*formül A*), if the child is born in a hospital. Otherwise, the child must be registered at the local registry office (*nufus müdürlüğu*).

Citizenship of Turkey is not automatic if a child is born in Turkey. The child does not always automatically receive citizenship of the parents' country either. Children of British parents, for example, must apply for registration at the British Embassy or Consulate and depending on where the parents were born citizenship and issuance of a full British passport is not automatic.

British parents need to follow the process outlined below and other nationalities should check the rules that will apply to their child with their own embassy.

The documents to be submitted, in person, to register a birth at the British Embassy are listed below. All documents are photocopied and returned immediately and the registration process then takes approximately three weeks.

- Completed 'Form of Application for the Registration of a Birth'.
- Turkish birth certificate (*formül A*).
- Hospital report.
- British passport of parent(s) with British nationality.
- Long birth certificate (for parents born after 1/1/1983), or naturalisation certificate of parent(s) with British nationality.
- Marriage certificate, declaration of paternity from both parents.
- Passport, or ID of non-British parent.
- Turkish ID of child (if already held).

Registration and other fees are payable in YTL at the British Consular rate of exchange applicable on the day of application:

- registration: £92;
- birth certificate: £59;
- passport for child under 16: £76.

For American citizens a Consular Report of Birth Abroad (CRBA) and passport for the child can be processed at the same time. The child and both parents need to be present at the time of the application. The documents required are listed below.

- Application for consular report of birth form.
- Application for social security number.
- Passport application form.
- Affidavit of parentage and physical presence form. The US citizen parent will need to sign this affidavit in the presence of the US consular officer.
- Two identical passport photographs.
- Turkish birth certificate (*formül A*).
- Parents' passports and two copies of each passport.
- Marriage certificate and one copy: translated if the certificate is not in English.
- Divorce decrees/death certificates to show termination of all prior marriages. The original and one copy of each document is needed, and a translation if the original certificate is not in English.
- Proof of previous physical presence in the USA for US citizen parents.

Registration and other fees are payable in US$, or by credit card at the Embassy:

- CRBA: US$65.00;
- passport: US$82.00.

Both parents should be present for the application, but if only one parent is able to appear, one of the following will be required in addition to the documents listed above:

- form DS-3053 (statement of consent) completed by the absent parent and notarised before a US or Turkish Notary Public (American Embassies and Consulates abroad can also notarise form DS-3053);
- copy of the absent parent's passport.

DEATH

Turkish death certificates are issued by the registry office (*nufus müdürluğu*). However, a death must be reported to the police in the first instance and the death certificate can only be issued if there are no suspicious circumstances relating to the death.

The British Embassy can issue a British death certificate on production of the Turkish equivalent and payment of a fee of approximately £150 payable in YTL at the consular rate of exchange on the date of payment.

Not all other Embassies charge a fee for issuing a death certificate, but all Embassies usually provide consular assistance to relatives and friends if one of their nationals dies in the country.

Repatriation of a body can be expensive and complicated and advice should be sought from your Embassy on the process. Cremation is unusual in Turkey and most funerals take place within 24 hours, as is customary in the Muslim faith.

Turkish funerals are more informal than Europeans and North Americans are used to and formal dress is not worn. The sexes will be segregated if the funeral is at a mosque.

INHERITANCE LAW

Wills drawn up outside of Turkey, by non-Turks resident in Turkey, will be recognised by Turkish courts, except in the case of any Turkish property owned by the deceased. Only where a directive is attached to the title deed (*tapu*) of the property in Turkey will the dispositions of the non-Turkish will be respected if it deviates from the rules laid down by Turkish law.

Additionally, any Turkish property must be referred to specifically by the non-Turkish will, rather than its assignation being merely implied.

In the event of a foreign resident dying without a valid last will and testament, Turkish inheritance law applies to all assets in Turkey, which will be disposed of in accordance with strict criteria. Turkish law dictates that there are reserved portions for various family members. A spouse cannot inherit a complete estate if an estate falls into Turkish jurisdiction due to a death without a will, or if a will was drawn up in Turkey under Turkish law. All debts are inherited by the estate and an inheritor is responsible for them unless they relinquish all rights to the inheritance.

Under Turkish inheritance laws children are the primary beneficiaries, receiving 75% of the estate, with the remaining 25% going to the spouse. For a childless couple, 50% goes to the spouse and the rest to the parents of the deceased. With no children or living parents, siblings of the deceased receive 25% and the spouse 75%. Where there are no children, surviving parents, or siblings, the entire estate will pass to the spouse. If the beneficiary is unable to own the property included in the estate, the property will be disposed of and the cash received then passed to beneficiary.

If there is no will and where no relatives can be traced, the estate passes to the government of Turkey.

For a Turkish will to be valid it must annotated by a Notary Public, or be handwritten, then lodged with a registry office. A will in this case must conform to Turkish law and any bequests must be made in line with the above-mentioned reservations to various relatives.

4
Accommodation

Finding somewhere to live is often time-consuming and stressful when moving to another country unless you are lucky enough to be moving to a job where the accommodation is available as part of your employment package.

Making sure that your accommodation is both suitable and safe is doubly important in Turkey, since the country is prone to frequent earthquakes. Istanbul and Izmir are both particularly susceptible to earthquakes and are common destinations for foreign residents; it is especially important here to make sure that the building you are planning to move into is structurally sound.

When looking for an apartment to rent, always ask for a structural report, which should be available from the building manager (*yönetıcı*).

Not many years ago, most of the coastal villages of Turkey were small isolated fishing communities. Then tourism arrived and over the last 20 years construction projects have boomed. Nowadays it can look like there are no old buildings left, but this is only partly due to the new construction projects, many of the older building have been destroyed in earthquakes.

One positive effect of the large earthquake of 1999 has been the improvement in, and greater enforcement of, building standards. The government has also made it mandatory to have earthquake insurance and leading insurance companies now offer cover on behalf of the government-backed scheme.

For Turks, the outward appearance of their buildings built since the Second World War was often less important than the interior, which means many buildings are drab and uninteresting. Gardens are not common either, especially in older properties. But as Turkey has grown more affluent and begun looking more towards Europe, and more Europeans have moved to the country, this is changing.

As new apartments and villas are being built for the burgeoning Turkish middle classes, and foreign buyers are looking for second homes, there is a growing trend to build traditional Mediterranean villas and apartment blocks and more luxurious and aesthetically-pleasing properties. These new properties often include gardens, swimming pools, sun terraces and designer exteriors.

Depending on where in Turkey you are looking for property, the style of the building and its environs will vary. In the centre of Istanbul, Ankara and Izmir the predominant options are apartments, but the further from the centre you go the more likely you are to find a house with a garden, or a communal development with open gardens and green areas for everyone to enjoy. In recent years garden suburbs along the lines of European and American developments have been appearing.

Along the coastal areas the new developments aimed at foreign buyers are more likely to be built in the 'villa' style, whether they are apartment blocks or individual properties. Many will also have a swimming pool and garden, or terrace area, though with many of the apartment blocks these areas will be communal.

There are a few areas where older buildings are available to buy. Parts of old Istanbul, Bursa and Antalya still have what are referred to as Ottoman buildings, but the areas are limited and the properties will often need extensive refurbishment. Older village houses are also available in the coastal areas of the Aegean and Mediterranean and some fine wood-built Ottoman houses have been bought and renovated by foreign buyers along the Black Sea coast in places like Safranbolu. These make fine boutique hotels, as well as being wonderful places in which to live.

Of the more exotic homes and properties bought by expatriates in Turkey, the cave dwellings in Cappadocia probably lead the way. Carved from the volcanic ash left by eruptions centuries ago, the houses, hotels and stables were slowly being abandoned in favour of above-ground structures offering an easier way of life. Tourism, though, has saved these incredible excavations from permanent abandonment. A favourite with Australians looking for an alternative business opportunity, there are now many foreign-owned guest houses and other tourism businesses in the area that complement the Turkish-owned properties which are now enjoying a renaissance.

RENTING PROPERTY

If you are looking to rent (*kiralik*) a house or apartment in Turkey there are a number of ways to find somewhere suitable and these are similar to the processes found in Europe and North America. Accommodation to rent will be advertised in newspapers, by word of mouth, or through letting agents (*emlakçı*).

If you are unfamiliar with the country, or lack Turkish language skills then using a letting agent could well be the easiest way to find suitable accommodation. Larger agents in popular expatriate areas advertise in the *Turkish Daily News* and are used to dealing with the requirements of foreigners, as well as being more likely to speak English.

The larger agents will probably deal in more expensive properties and if you are on a limited budget then using a local agent based in your preferred area will be more likely to yield results in your price range.

Agents' fees are standard for the tenant, but the amount payable is negotiable, just like the rent, especially if it is paid in US$ or Euros. Hard bargaining can yield good discounts and be well worth the effort. Also negotiable are the currency of payments, terms of the lease, redecoration of the property and the electrical appliances to be provided in the kitchen. As when you are negotiating for rented accommodation anywhere in the world, get any promises from the landlord in writing before handing over any money. Also consider getting a lawyer to check the contract and make sure you have a break clause so you can terminate the lease if you have to leave the country, move city, or want to upgrade to somewhere better.

The rent will usually not include the cost of utilities, shared facilities (e.g. swimming pool), odd job man (*kapıcı*) salary, or environment tax (*çevre ve temizlik vergisi*), but will cover major repairs and ongoing maintenance.

If you have the budget to do so, then using a relocation agent to help you find somewhere suitable to live can be well worth the investment. A good agent will make sure you get a property within your budget, near the facilities and amenities you need and ensure that the contract and all other matters relating to the property, such as utilities, are sorted out before you arrive. This will greatly reduce the stress of moving and make the transition a much more enjoyable process.

A good relocation agent will also arrange additional services such as setting up registration with a doctor who speaks your language, schools for your children, language classes and an orientation tour of your destination city.

BUYING PROPERTY

The Turkish property market has been booming in recent years. This boom has been driven as much by foreigners looking for second homes as by newly-affluent Turks upgrading and entrepreneurs looking for investment property or a business opportunity.

Unlike in many countries, the buyer of a property is usually liable for the agent's fees and this can lead to the idea that the agent is working for the buyer and there is no need for a lawyer to be involved: this is not the case. Legal advice should always be sought when buying property in Turkey, just as when you buy property in your home country. Just because the sun is shining and everybody is welcoming and friendly is no reason to forget that this is a business transaction involving a lot of money.

Historically, the Turkish property market has been restricted to domestic buyers, but since 2003 the market has been liberalised and in January 2006, as part of the drive towards entry into the EU, foreign buyers were given equal rights to buy property in Turkey as long as there is reciprocity with their home country.

Prices have risen sharply for new properties in areas popular with foreign buyers, but extensive ongoing building projects are likely to impact on this growth and much of the rises can also be put down to improved building standards since the 1999 earthquake.

Turkey is a land of contrasts and the property market is no exception. While Turkey is often thought of as a poor country, there are many wealthy families and successful professional people with money to spend. It is not uncommon for houses along the Bosphorus in Istanbul to sell for far more than £1m and Turks have long had favourite holiday home destinations that are often not on the map for foreign visitors, but where property can be as expensive as in more mainstream European countries.

Turkish estate agents are common. In the tourist areas they may well specialise in selling retirement properties, holiday homes and investment properties to international clients, whilst in areas where expatriates are looking for somewhere to live while working in the country, the property agents will deal with both Turkish and foreign clients.

When buying property in Turkey it is necessary to factor in the cost of completing the transaction over and above the purchase price of the property itself. The agent's commission payable by the buyer is usually 3%, while the transfer tax of 3% is usually split between buyer and seller. Legal fees can be lower than Europe and North America, but will still be in the region of £1,000 by the time notary fees and translation costs have been taken into account. There is more information on costs on page 70.

The legal process is straightforward and there are unlikely to be issues concerning the ownership of a property as the land registration process is well regulated and registration of a property sale is mandatory under law. Once the process is complete the title deed (*tapu*) passes to the new owner immediately.

A good solicitor will carry out a number of steps to determine that the seller legally owns the property, that the correct planning permissions and consents are in place and that the property is not in an area where foreigners cannot buy property. The solicitor should also check that there are no outstanding charges or taxes on the property, because the buyer will become liable for them once the sale goes through.

Though the property market has been liberalised there are still some restrictions on where non-Turks can buy property. For national security reasons foreigners cannot buy property near a designated military zone. To prevent property speculation and retain affordability for local residents, property cannot be bought outside an urban municipality (*belediye*).

Once a sale is agreed and all the mandatory checks have been done it is standard practice to agree a contract of sale that includes details of the property, deposit and sale price, fixtures and fittings included in the sale and who will pay the taxes and fees. Other details may be included depending on the particular sale. Contracts are often notarised to ensure they are legal and binding. For foreign buyers it is worth having an official translation included in the notarisation to reduce the chance of arguments later.

Upon signing of the contract of sale a military and police check is carried out on the purchaser to ensure they are fit to own property in Turkey. This process can take months to complete, though fortunately it does not always take so long. If you pass this check and are cleared to make the purchase by the police, the sale can be completed, the *tapu* transferred at the land registry (*tapu dairesi*) and payment of the agreed price made. The buyer and seller must both be present and, if the property is jointly owned or is to be bought by two or more people, all buyers or sellers as appropriate must be present. If someone cannot be present then their designated agent, usually a solicitor with power of attorney, can represent them.

The sale must be registered at the municipality (*belediye*) by the end of the year in which the sale takes place and the transfer tax, based on the declared sale price, paid at this time. Under-declaration of purchase prices is common in Turkey so that people can pay a reduced amount of tax, but the government is expected to clamp down on this process and impose hefty fines on tax-evaders.

Property tax, paid bi-annually, is based on the declared sale price. If the seller under-declared the value during their purchase process they will be keen to do so again at the point they sell the property so as to avoid a liability for capital gains tax.

Under Turkish law anyone caught avoiding the transfer tax and subsequent property tax by under-declaring the sale price can be fined, have to pay the evaded tax and interest on the underpaid tax at approximately 35% per annum from the point of evasion. For residential buildings the annual property tax is 0.3%, but in some municipalities (e.g. Ankara, Istanbul, Antalya and Izmir) it is double the standard rate.

PURCHASE COSTS

Apart from the purchase price of the property there are always additional costs, fees and expenses. In Turkey these costs can be up to 10% of the purchase price.

As previously detailed, agents' fees are generally 3% of the agreed sale price and are the responsibility of the buyer. The property transfer tax is an additional 3% of the declared sale price, which is usually split equally between the buyer and seller. The tax is due before the final transfer of ownership and registration. For a new build property the tax is 1.5% paid by the buyer only. Some sellers will try and make the buyer pay all the tax, but this should be resisted.

In certain circumstances VAT is chargeable on a property transaction (e.g. at an auction). For properties of less than 150m^2 the rate is 1.5% and for properties of more than 150m^2 the rate jumps massively to 18%.

Professional fees and costs for solicitors, public notary and translators can be up to £1,000 (US$2,000), with the public notary and translators fees often due immediately at the point of notarisation. If you are not present at the exchange of paperwork it will be necessary to sign a power of attorney to authorise your solicitor to complete the transaction for you, which incurs an additional cost.

While not technically a property purchase cost, earthquake insurance is mandatory and will need to be purchased at the point of purchase from one of a number of private insurance companies. This insurance is underwritten by the government. Connections of water and electricity services will cost approximately an additional £250 (US$500) and the procedure for arranging this is detailed below.

UTILITIES

Everywhere, except in isolated areas, there will be easy connection to mains water and electricity. However, the power can be subject to significant variations and outages and the water, whilst it is safe to drink, it is not always pleasant due to chlorination.

If you are moving in to a previously occupied property the mains services will usually be connected already and a transfer of account into your name is all that will be required. This will need to be done in person at the local office of the particular supplier and should take no more than lots of patience and a day of your time.

All utility bills can be paid by direct debit, though they can also be paid monthly at the utility company office and at some banks.

Gas

Most people use bottled gas, except in Istanbul, central Ankara and a few other major towns where there is a piped mains supply. In apartment blocks the caretaker (*kapıcı*) will usually bring you a new bottle and connect it as and when needed, elsewhere the bottles will be delivered regularly. They can also be readily purchased from retail outlets.

Electricity

TEDAŞ supply electricity at 220V and 50Hz, and the Turkish standard connection is a round-pin two prong plug. European standard plugs will work in Turkish sockets and vice-versa. German and Turkish plugs are interchangeable, though not all French plugs are due to the presence of the permanent earth pin of some French sockets.

UK appliances will work in Turkey, but electrical products are easily available in Turkey and local makes include the well-known European brand, Beko, in addition to Arçelik and Profilo. Surge protectors are a good investment for delicate equipment such as computers, but a UPS (uninterruptible power supply) is essential for computers if you are to avoid the frustrations of lost work and damaged equipment.

Water

The mains water supply is organised by the municipality (*belediye*) and is metered and billed inclusive of an environmental tax. Drinking water will generally be delivered to your door in 20 litre bottles that are suitable for dispensers and chiller units that are sold in most hardware and electrical stores.

COMMUNICATIONS

Telephone

Fixed line phone services are provided by Türk Telecom and a personal visit of many hours to their office will often be required to secure the service. The process is frustrating and time-consuming, but generally will result in a telephone line being connected within days of you completing the registration process.

Various tariffs are available depending on your usage, but unless you specify at the time you sign up for your line the default will be the standard line (*standartHATT*) service. The various services, costs and explanations can be found, in English, on the Turk Telecom website: www.turktelekom.com.tr/eng_default.asp.

As telephone handsets from outside Turkey are not always compatible, it is advisable to plan on buying a new handset in the country. There is a wide choice available in Turkey and finding one to suit your needs, as well as your sense of taste and style, should not be too difficult.

Internet

Email and internet services are widely available through cable TV and fixed telephone line services. The availability of cable TV is limited in coverage to certain regions, but will be available in most central areas of the big cities where working expatriates live. If you are living in smaller towns, the suburbs or on the coast you may need to find an alternative service provision.

For fixed phone line connections to the internet, a Türk Telecom telephone line will be needed, as well as the subscription to an internet service provider. Dial-up and broadband connections are available from a number of providers, though broadband is often no more expensive, and will certainly be more useful, than a dial-up service.

In addition to Türk Telecom, there are other internet service providers as listed in Appendix A.

Mobile Phones

There are three providers of mobile phone (*çep*) services (see Appendix A for further information) in Turkey. Handsets are widely available from the retail outlets of the service providers, as well as elsewhere. Avea and Turkcell both have English language sections on their websites, where information on the various tariffs and services are available. The Vodafone site at this time is totally in Turkish. Both pre-paid (pay-as-you-go) and contract services are available, and a subscription to any service requires a passport. For a contract service you will also need to have secured your residence permit.

Non-Turkish mobile phones with a roaming facility will work in Turkey, but there are usually high charges and it is often cheaper to acquire a Turkish mobile phone if your usage is going to be more than occasional. Detailed information on roaming charges incurred in Turkey will be available from the service provider in your home country.

Under a law introduced in Turkey in 2005, mobile phones must be registered centrally so that they can be disabled if they are stolen. This means that a mobile phone brought into Turkey and used in conjunction with a Turkish service provider's sim card will also need to be registered. You will need to provide your proof of purchase as well as the identity number of the phone in order to register it. If you attempt to use the phone without registering it, it will be blocked and unusable thereafter in Turkey.

TELEVISION AND DVD

Televisions and DVDs in Turkey are compatible with the PAL system and UK standard equipment will work with a Turkish mains plug or adapter. Some European and all American televisions and DVDs are not generally compatible unless they have a multi-system capability.

The usual broadcasting options of free-to-air, cable and satellite services are available in Turkey, though cable services are restricted to certain, mainly urban, areas.

Cine 5 (Cine beş), Digitürk and Turk Telecom offer cable services, but they only offer a few limited English channels such as CNN, BBC Prime and BBC World.

Satellite services are more extensive in their coverage and it is possible to receive European broadcasts in some western areas of the country to supplement the Turkish service, assuming you have a satellite receiver set up for the European providers.

The free-to-air Turkish channels are broadcast by TRT, a state-owned broadcaster which provides few non-Turkish programmes. Satellite and cable broadcasters are private organisations and are a better option if you are looking for a wider choice of channels, including ones in English and other languages.

POSTAL SERVICES

The mail service is state run and deliveries will often arrive at destinations outside of Turkey faster than within Turkey, especially if express, as opposed to standard, service is used. In apartment blocks it is not uncommon for the mail to be delivered centrally and the *kapıcı* to distribute it, or place it in individual mailboxes in the central lobby. Parcels will be left near the mail boxes, or kept in the *kapıcı*'s office until you collect them.

If you live in a house, or an apartment without a *kapıcı*, then parcels will be delivered directly to your address, but not left outside if you are out. If you miss a delivery it will be necessary to visit the parcel office, often referred to as *gumruk*, to collect your delivery in person. Though the system is improving, the process can be fraught and you will need your passport, the notification slip and a lot of patience before the parcel is handed over. The office is also likely to be in some isolated part of town and difficult to find. As it is possible for someone else to collect your parcel if they have a copy of your passport and the delivery slip, this can be the preferred route to claiming your parcel.

Outgoing mail can be posted at any Turkish Post Office (Postane), which is usually signified by PTT signs, but may also be marked with a Türk Telecom sign. Offices are numerous and can easily be found in most city areas, as well as in towns and villages. Main offices (*merkez postanesi*) offer *post restante* services in towns, and some smaller offices, especially away from the big cities, also offer the service.

International redirection services are available from post offices in many countries and this can prove very useful to ensure all your mail follows you when you move to Turkey.

Courier Services

Private courier and mail services also operate in Turkey, with intra-city, inter-city and international operations available. For quick and secure transfer of documents and parcels Istanbul, Ankara and Izmir have many domestic operators, a few of them also have a network of offices around the country. Some of the leading private bus companies also offer an intercity cargo service.

5
Daily Living

The major aspects of living abroad, like work and accommodation, though time-consuming to arrange, often remain stable for much of the time spent living in the country and as such have a predictable and known impact on your life.

On the other hand, the small things in daily living can be unpredictable, frustrating and confusing on a regular basis. Without advance preparation and continued management, it is often the ongoing little annoyances of life that can make living in a foreign country an unpleasant experience as they become magnified out of proportion.

Planning, preparation and management of your expectations, both before relocating and after arrival, will drastically influence how you ultimately feel about living 'away from home'.

LANGUAGE

Being able to speak the local language is always advantageous, even knowing a few words when you arrive will go a long way towards helping you settle in to your new home. Learning a new language is only easy for a small number of people, but with some effort and a willingness to practise then a lot can be achieved.

Turkish is not the easiest language for Europeans to learn, as it is not an Indo-European language. However, the Turks are helpful and encouraging when you make the effort and usually make every attempt to understand what you are trying to say.

Turkish is spoken throughout the country by the vast majority of the population, though there are a number of minority languages spoken too – Armenian, Greek, Kurdish and Laz. Many Turks have also lived in Germany and German is the unofficial second language, whereas English is encouraged in the school system.

Around the Aegean and Mediterranean coasts a lot of staff in the tourism sector will speak English and/or German and it is not uncommon to find at least one English speaker in even the remotest village. In the big cities of Izmir, Ankara and Istanbul many professional, middle class Turks have studied abroad, or attended one of the English-medium Turkish universities, and will also speak English. Even so, being able to communicate effectively in Turkish greatly enhances the experience of living in Turkey.

There are several ways to learn Turkish. Self study is one that many people try, but while it is usually a good introduction it is often the least successful in building a competent level of communication skills. Classroom lessons and personal instruction are a much more focused way to learn – as long as the teaching is of an adequate standard.

Self-Study Course

The traditional method of teaching yourself Turkish – using a book, pen and paper – is still available, but the use of either a CD or CD-ROM in conjunction with a book has become increasingly popular.

The CD method is broadly similar to now-superseded, tape-based courses and offers the chance to learn and practise on the move, particularly if you have some privacy to allow you to try out pronunciation.

Use of a CD-ROM often requires a fixed location to use a computer or other electronic device, but can be a much more interactive and flexible way to learn.

Self-study courses are often available at good bookshops, especially larger outlets. Alternatively they can be purchased directly from publishers' websites, from the author's website, or from online retailers.

An emerging medium for instruction is the internet. There are also a few websites offering online tuition, with varying amounts of interactivity and fee levels. Examples of self-study courses are listed in Appendix A.

Classroom Courses

Outside Turkey, classes are available at educational institutions in large cities and sometimes they are also offered under the auspices of the Turkish Embassy. Local searches for Turkish Associations can be a good way to find classes as well as enquiries at local colleges. Details of a few organisations offering courses are listed in Appendix A, though there will be many local organisations offering additional options.

Classroom courses in Turkey are available in many places, particularly where foreigners live and work, or visit on holiday. Istanbul, Izmir, Ankara and Antalya offer lots of choice from companies offering one-to-one tuition to university-level courses for those who want to progress their skills beyond simple conversation. Elsewhere the level of provision will be based on current demand, though, if you can find enough people who want to learn, then establishing your own class should not prove difficult. The best-known courses are listed in Appendix A, but there are many more available.

Private Tuition

An equally popular and often much more convenient way to learn Turkish is to arrange a private tutor. With the advantage of only having to find a mutually convenient time and place for two people to meet, as opposed to a whole class, there is a much wider variety of locations and times available.

Whether the arrangement comes about through a personal recommendation of a private tutor, or is an arrangement between friends, there are lots of options when arranging private tuition that can be mutually beneficial.

CULTURE

Cultural training courses go beyond providing language lessons, and cover social and business etiquette, local customs and the cultural context of the country. It is increasingly common for organisations sending staff abroad to provide such training and it is well worth trying to involve other family members as well.

EDUCATION

The Turkish education system is well developed, with education available from pre-school to post-graduate level. Full-time education is free in state schools and is compulsory for eight years of primary education, which includes three years of what is known as secondary education in the UK and Middle School in the USA.

Classroom sizes are large in the state system with an average size of 50 pupils, though the government has an ongoing programme to reduce this to 30. Foreign languages (French, German or English) are taught in the last three years of the compulsory system to all pupils and increasing numbers of native speakers are delivering these lessons.

There are many private schools around the country, including a number delivering an international curriculum, as well as a number of schools sponsored by various diplomatic missions, particularly in Ankara and Istanbul.

The leading international curriculum is the International Baccalaureate, delivered by schools on behalf of the International Baccalaureate Organisation (IBO – www.ibo.org). The IBO has its headquarters in Switzerland and works through offices around the world, with over 2,000 schools in 125 countries. The curriculum has three main programmes and covers the age range from 3 to 18 and leads to the IB Diploma, which is a world-recognised award for university entrance.

A British-based international curriculum is run by the Cambridge University Examination Board as Cambridge International Examinations (CIE), which offers programmes in more than 200 schools around the world, covering the age range 5 to 18. At 16 years of age students sit the International General Certificate of Education (IGCSE) exams and for students who pass seven exams, from a broad range of subjects, there is the International Certificate of Education (ICE) award. At age 18 students would sit A and/or AS Level exams and those who gain a total of six credits (A Level = 2, AS = 1) are awarded an Advanced International Certificate of Education (AICE). This award is offered by schools in Florida as well as other countries around the world and is accepted by US as well as UK and British Commonwealth universities. US university students often gain advanced credits on the basis of their AICE.

While not really offering an international curriculum, a number of schools offer a US Curriculum accredited by one of the main accreditation bodies in the US. This allows students to transfer to another US-style school and take credits earned with them and also have their high school diploma recognised by US universities. Some IB and CIE schools also have a US accreditation.

International Schools in Turkey

There are 23 schools offering all or part of the International Baccalaureate (www.ibo.org) programme depending on the age ranges of the school. Additionally there are 23 schools in Turkey which are members of ECIS (European Council of International Schools; www.ecis.org).

US Accredited Schools in Turkey

Only two schools are accredited by the US organisation, New England Association of Schools and Colleges (www.neasc.org), with one more going through the accreditation process.

University Education

Turkey is well served with state universities, but they are over-subscribed. This has led to a number of private universities opening, often teaching in English, and recruiting international lecturers.

More than 50 universities operate across the country and students gain entry through a centrally-administered entrance examination. Even the private universities are part of this system, which ranks students according to their mark in the exam and then allocates students to their preferred course if it is available. Students lower down the ranking are often allocated to courses and universities that still have vacancies, even though they have no desire to study that subject in that particular city.

To increase their scores, students attend special crammer courses (*derşane*), either at night school, or for a full year after leaving high school. Foreign students, primarily from the Turkic republics, who wish to attend a Turkish university sit a separate exam that measures their ability in both Turkish and English.

Increasingly, Turkish families with the resources to do so send their children abroad to study. The USA has historically been a popular destination, but Europe is becoming more popular as it is seen as closer and safer.

All of the universities in Turkey are overseen by the Council of Higher Education (Türkiye Cumhurriyet Yükseköğretim Kurulu – YÖK) and links to the websites of the various universities listed in Appendix A can be found on the YÖK website at: http://www.yok.gov.tr/english/oku22.html.

JUDICIAL SYSTEM

For many foreigners, crime levels seem very low and only in certain parts of Istanbul is petty crime a real problem. In many parts of the country if you leave something behind in a restaurant someone will run after you to return it.

The only time many people find themselves in trouble and dealing with the authorities is for speeding in a car, and then the process can be remarkably quick as fines can often be paid on the spot at checkpoints.

When Atatürk set up the Republic he created a new legal system which, in keeping with his social reforms, he linked closely to the European model. The legislators drew extensively on the French and Swiss legal codes, and the legislation of certain other European countries for specific areas of law, such as the UK for prevention of terrorism legislation. Turkey has also joined the European Court of Human Rights and is a signatory to the bulk of the European Convention on Human Rights.

The legal system has long been independent of the government and fiercely protects the legal process from attempts by governments to operate outside the constitution. As Turkey proceeds along the slow path towards full EU membership it has modified certain legislation to bring it closer in line with Europe, including abolishing the death penalty.

Overseeing the judicial system is the Constitutional Court (*Anayasa*) that ensures the government and the lower courts operate within the law and that legislation is properly implemented and respected. Never shy of taking major decisions, in 2007 the Constitutional Court ruled that parliament had not voted correctly in selecting the president and forced a general election.

Below the Constitutional Court are a number of other courts that are responsible for specific areas of law, or have specific responsibilities, much as in the British judicial system.

The Council of State (*Danıştay*) operates in much the same way as the Law Lords in the UK and rules on major cases where the outcome of the case could affect future judicial rulings of courts lower down the system.

The Appeals Court (*Yargıtay*) is the final arbiter of cases heard by the lower courts once appeals in those courts have been exhausted.

The Haciz Courts rule on administrative issues in the various regions and along with the Court of Accounts (*Sayıştay*), which audits government spending, is unlikely to affect foreign residents directly.

The Military Courts only deal with military personnel, except during emergency rule (such as after a coup) when civilians can be tried in a military court for crimes committed against the state.

Police activity is split between urban and rural areas, with separate forces acting in the two areas. The Turkish national police (*polis*), under the jurisdiction of the Ministry of the Interior, look after the urban areas, whilst in the rural areas, that make up the vast majority of the land area of the country, the *jandarma*, who report to the military as well as the civil authorities, are in control.

Police activity is high across Turkey and all police officers always carry a gun, with the *jandarma* being particularly heavily armed as they are a paramilitary force which has also been used extensively in operations against the PKK in the south east of the country. When they believe it is necessary, the police will act decisively and forcefully and water cannon are always in evidence at large demonstrations. That being said, the Turkish police are friendly and helpful and likely to give you a smile as they move their gun out of the way as you walk past.

Traffic police are also visible and active on the chaotic roads and will stop motorists and impose fines in what can seem a random fashion. A visit to the police station to pay a fine is to be avoided if at all possible because of the length of time required to complete the process, so if there's an option for an on-the-spot fine: take it!

Crimes should be reported to the local office of the *polis* or *jandarma* as appropriate, who will provide theft or other reports as necessary for insurance purposes.

Turkey takes seriously any perceived slight against the country and it is a criminal offence to insult the flag, the country or Atatürk, as more than a few visiting football fans have found to their cost.

SOCIAL LIFE

A good social life and interaction with host nationals can make living abroad a wonderful and fulfilling experience. Fortunately, the Turks are sociable, friendly and welcoming and the biggest problem can be knowing which invitations to accept and which to decline. Turkey is also very family- and child-friendly, so it is not always necessary to find a babysitter as children are always welcome.

Whether meeting at a restaurant, or in someone's home the level of hospitality and welcome will be overwhelming and provided to the best quality the host can afford. Food will be in abundance and come with an expectation that you will eat everything put in front of you.

In the summer barbecues (*oçak başı*) are popular and can last all day, with a steady stream of courses and dishes being cooked by the host. In the barbecue restaurants a little brazier will be brought to your table so you can cook your food to your own taste.

From the European borders of Greece and Bulgaria in the west to the Georgian, Iranian, Armenian, Syrian and Iraqi borders in the east, the social customs change with the shift in culture, but wherever you are hospitality is the watchword.

If you are working or studying in Turkey you will have a ready-made introduction to colleagues and a social life. If you have retired then it will take time and effort to meet people, but there are expat clubs as well as social activities for locals that will provide plenty of opportunity to meet people.

When greeting someone in Turkey there is always a ritual to go through.

> *Merhaba* (hello)
>
> *Nasılsınız?* (How are you?)
>
> *Iyim* (Fine)
>
> *Siz nasılsınız?* (How are you?)

If you are visiting someone, or arrive at a party, the host will greet you formally too, for which there is a specific response.

> *Hoş geldiniz* (Welcome)
>
> *Hoş bulduk* (Pleased to be here)

When visiting it is traditional to take a small gift for your host, such as chocolates or something from the many patisseries selling the sugary cakes that Turks love so much. Alcohol is rarely given, especially early in a friendship.

Once you know someone better the formal language will slip to the informal, as with French. It is always better to follow the lead of your Turkish friends and wait for them to make the transition to informality first.

Friends of the same sex, as opposed to acquaintances, will greet each other with a kiss on each cheek, though more cosmopolitan Turks will also greet friends of the opposite sex with a kiss too.

RELIGION – CHURCHES, SYNAGOGUES, ETC.

Though it is an overwhelmingly Muslim country, Turkey has a hugely important place in Christian and Jewish history too. The country is officially a secular republic with freedom of religion and there are active mosques, churches and synagogues offering services on a weekly basis.

All mosques come under state control and receive their funding from a government department.

The Muslim population is dominant and there are many thousands of mosques throughout the country serving the devout Muslims who attend the call to prayer. Foreign residents will be well aware of Ramadan, Eid and other major events in the Muslim calendar, but other than restaurants closing during the day and people being a bit short-tempered during the daytime fasts, foreigners will not be greatly affected.

However, there are many middle-class and professional Turks who are as religious as their counterparts in England, resulting in the mosques being noticeably busier during Ramadan and during religious festivals. The relaxed attitude to religion is evident in the fact that beer is the favourite national drink and the strong aniseed liquor, *rakı*, is available everywhere and drunk regularly by many Turkish men – resulting in some Turks giving up alcohol and cigarettes for Ramadan, just as some Europeans give up chocolate and sugar for Lent.

Unlike in a number of other Muslim countries non-Muslims are welcome in mosques outside of prayer times. If you are respectfully dressed there will usually be no issue with entering to view the stunning architecture and rich history contained in the mosques of villages and towns throughout the country. It is worth remembering though that if you walk in front of someone who is praying they will have to restart their prayers.

RELIGIOUS AND PUBLIC HOLIDAYS

Turkey adopted the Western calendar at the start of the Republican era, but the Islamic calendar is still followed for many important holidays, which means the dates of the holidays change every year. Only the state holidays are fixed and these include:

- New Year's Day;
- National Day (also called Children's Day – Çoçuk Bayram), April 23;
- Atatürk Day, May 19;
- Victory Day, August 30;
- Republic Day, October 29th (afternoon of October 28th also a holiday).

The religious (moveable) holidays include:

Ramadan – The month long period of daylight fasting which occurs 11 days earlier than the year before. The country is noticeably quieter during this period, particularly the restaurants during daylight hours.

Şeker Bayram – The sugar festival follows immediately after Ramadan, but is not an official holiday. The adult population seems to ply every child they know with copious amounts of sweet and sugary food making the children hyperactive and unable to sleep. The noise levels in restaurants and other meeting places is very high at this time of the year.

Kubram Bayram – The Feast of the Sacrifice is a significant religious festival involving the ritual and public slaughter of the biggest animal a family can afford, some of which is then given to those in need.

Christian festivals are not celebrated and Christmas is a normal working day, though Christmas trees and decorations appear in December and presents are exchanged at New Year. It is a widely held belief in Turkey that Santa Claus came from the village of Demre, on the Turkish Mediterranean coast, and you will be reminded of this frequently.

Fethiye Oludeniz coast and beach

View of Antalya old town

Night view of Istanbul

'The Great Theatre' at Ephesus

Turkish bread with
sesame seeds: *simit*

Archeological site in Perge

Caravanserai on the Silk Route

Cave city in Cappadocia

St. Simeon Church and houses, Pasa Baglari, Cappadocia

Turkish coffee

Historical windmills in Datca

© 2008 yusuf anil akduygu/iStock

Night view of Bosphorus Bridge

© 2008 George Cairns/iStock

Fairy chimneys in Pasabag, Cappadocia

© 2007 Andree Feurich/iStock

Mosque at Taurus mountains

TURKISH FOOD

The Turks love their food and though it is very similar to Greek food, due to the shared history and the population exchanges of the 1920s, the Turks will proclaim it is the best in the Mediterranean. Whether it is home prepared, or cooked fresh in a restaurant, the range of flavours and the diversity of dishes around the country makes contradicting their claims difficult.

Restaurants usually specialise in certain foods, which can be as limited as one dish such as in *lahmaçun* and *pide* (flat dough bases covered in spicy meat or vegetable toppings) establishments, or one species such as in fish (*balık*) restaurants. Kebab restaurants are ubiquitous, but the variety is bewildering as you move around the country. In the large cities some restaurants specialise in regional food, reflecting the home town of the owner.

Most restaurants offer starters (*meze*), similar in nature to Spanish tapas, when you will have the chance to sample sheep's brain and other offal carefully prepared to tempt unwary visitors before they realise what is on the plate in front of them.

It will be noticeable to people living in the country that food in the shops is highly seasonal, which for those moving from Europe and North America will be something of a shock. Even the meat and the milk will change flavour as the seasons change and the grass goes from green to brown.

To accompany your food there is always a wide range of fruit juices including cherry (*vişne*), peach (*şeftali*) and orange (*portakal*).

Beer is the most popular drink in Turkey and there are a number of home-produced varieties such as Efes, Tuborg, Venus, as well as imported European and American brands.

Wine has been produced for centuries in a number of areas. Though not all are of brilliant quality, there are some great wines, both red and white, from Cappadocia, Thrace and Ankara among others. Though imported wines are available, the high prices prove a disincentive and makes drinking Turkish wines the sensible option.

MEDIA

Turkey has a robust and lively media, with an abundance of local newspapers and private TV channels. International magazines and newspapers are also available in the larger towns and cities and tourist destinations. Satellite television services add to the mix.

Newspapers

There are three national English language publications in Turkey, the long-standing *Turkish Daily News* (www.turkishdailynews.com.tr) now facing competition from *Today's Zaman* (www.todayszaman.com) and *The Turkish Herald* (www.theturkishherald.com). The major Turkish language newspaper, *Hurriyet*, also has an English language website (www.hurriyet.com.tr/english/).

To complement the national publications there are a number of local English language offerings for resident expats, mostly retirees, along the coast. *Didim Today* (www.didimtoday.com), *Turkish Riviera News* (http://turkishrivieranews.com/) and *Voices Newspaper* (www.voicesnewspaper.com) are prominent, but this is likely to change as the market develops.

Television

Television broadcasts, DVDs and videos in Turkey are all in the UK equivalent PAL format and DVDs are Region 2 compatible.

There are satellite, cable and free-to-air (received via a roof-top aerial) options for receiving television, but they are not all available in all areas and local research will be necessary to determine what will be best in each location. See page 74 for more information.

As internet broadcasting develops there are more services available online and it is becoming increasingly common to be able to watch, or listen to, your favourite TV or radio programme from the other side of the world. The internet may be the best way in some areas to keep up with international news and entertainment.

6
Working in Turkey

Working abroad is always a different proposition from working in your home country. Many of the basic rules are different in a foreign country and can make the new environment more difficult to cope with than would be the case if you started a new job at home.

The cultural differences of the country will cause culture shock in relation to your work. The differences manifest themselves both in your relationships with colleagues and business associates and how business is actually conducted.

CULTURAL ISSUES

To the surprise of many foreign nationals, women have broadly similar rights to men in the workplace in Turkey and have risen to senior positions in many companies and organisations, in both the private and public sector.

There is equal access to education, up to university level, and selection for university places is purely on merit. Turkey has had a female Prime Minister and the head of one of the largest family companies in the country won the job against competition from male relatives.

Respect

One of the main cultural drivers in the workplace is respect for your elders, which can take precedence over rank in certain circumstances and should always be considered when asking for advice or information from local staff. In some circumstances a more senior-ranking employee may defer to one who is older, which can be particularly frustrating if they have agreed to do something for you and are then overruled by the older person.

Social rank is also an important consideration and can be difficult to overcome as some staff will always defer to someone of perceived higher social class, despite their position or role in the company. This can be so ingrained that if foreign staff, who are generally regarded as having a higher social position, socialise publicly with lower grade local staff then those local staff can gain the disapproval of colleagues for trying to rise above their situation. Care should, therefore, be taken to consider the implications of your actions and you may do well to limit where and when you socialise and with whom, even if this goes against the grain.

Turks will often dress more informally than many expatriates would do, even when attending what are traditionally formal occasions for Europeans, such as weddings and business functions. However, it is often wise to overdress until you are familiar with the local business etiquette. It is always easier to dress down by loosening a tie or removing a jacket than to find a way of smartening up.

Dress

The style of dress in the main Turkish cities of Ankara, Izmir and Istanbul is the same as in cities further north in Europe. Women will wear fashionable and recognisably designer clothes and men will wear expensive suits and silk ties: you would be hard pressed to realise you were not in any major European city. The further east and the more rural you go, though, the more conservative the dress code and the more women, in particular, will feel that long sleeves and lower hemlines are more suitable. The style of clothes also become more Turkish.

Time Keeping

Time-keeping is the opposite of the northern European countries and follows the more relaxed Mediterranean style, with late arrivals, or even missed appointments, not uncommon. However, when a meeting does take place there is a ritual that is almost rigidly followed, with the host providing tea or coffee with (*orta*) or without (*sade*) sugar.

The importance of personal relationships

The progression of a meeting also has its own etiquette that is similar to that found in the Middle East. As personal relationships are important in business, coming directly to the point in a business meeting is considered impolite. Sometimes long conversations are required about the health of family, friends, sport or other subjects before the subject in hand can be comfortably raised. Efforts to speed the conversation along, and hurry up the process, is likely to offend your Turkish customer or partner and has the potential to scupper your long-term business aspirations. Learning to relax and go with the flow will get you a long way in Turkey.

The development and importance of personal relationships in business has the advantage that such relationships can become long term, and parties are willing to work through any difficulties that may arise, rather that break the relationship off at the first hint of trouble or the first offer of a cheaper competitive product. This does mean, though, that it can take some time to initiate a business relationship as the prospective buyer wants to make sure the seller really is someone that they want to do business with.

Due to the strong sense of national identity and pride in the country and its heritage, criticism of the country by anyone, especially a foreign national, is not well received and could prove fatal to any business relationship. This is even more so if the criticism is aimed at the founder of the Republic, Kemal Atatürk, whose picture appears in almost every office and public space.

DOING BUSINESS IN TURKEY

As in many other countries where personal relationships are important in business, small and inconsequential deals are often made first to see how the interaction takes place and to ensure that both partners are honourable, before larger deals are entered into. These small orders may initially seem not worth the bother, but such a test can prove well worth the investment in the future.

Networking and the use of networks is a finely developed aspect of doing business in Turkey. Once you have developed a good business partnership, the potential for further business comes from being introduced to their contacts of close and distant relatives, friends from their home town or region and their looser network of other business associates. This aspect of doing business in Turkey should never be underestimated and asking for an introduction to someone from a close contact is often the best way to expand your business.

Turks are very sociable and hospitable and will combine this with work by inviting business associates to family events. Summer barbecues are especially popular and may be attended by large numbers of friends and family. Many hours can be spent developing the social side of a business relationship in this way.

WORK OPPORTUNITIES FOR EXPATRIATES

The Turkish economy is well-developed and, compared to some parts of Europe, the manufacturing sector is still particularly strong. Other important areas of the economy are the financial and banking sector, the construction industry and the education sector. Tourism is particularly strong and growing year on year.

With relatively little in the way of a social welfare system, education is sought after and families expect children to work hard at school. There is a strong merit driven education sector, that is highly competitive at university level, and this has produced a Turkish workforce which is well educated.

The limited social welfare system promotes entrepreneurship, ambition and hard work, whilst keeping wages low. Turkish families consider education important and children are encouraged to study hard and look internationally to gain the best qualifications they can. This has resulted in large numbers studying abroad and gaining language skills, especially in German and English, to complement their more standard qualifications.

As a foreigner can only be employed if no Turkish national can do the job, direct employment for foreigners can be limited as there will often be any number of Turks able and willing to do most jobs. This will generally be for much less money than an equivalently-skilled foreigner would consider anyway.

Teaching

Some sectors, however, offer very good prospects for foreign staff; education being a prime example. English language skills are highly valued and this has produced strong demand for qualified EFL teachers across the country, from big cities in the west, to remote towns in the east.

A step up from EFL teaching are the mainstream schools where English language instruction is part of the curriculum. In the private schools English is the medium of instruction and subject-specific teachers (e.g. maths, history, science, literature, etc.) with mother tongue English language skills are required in addition to English as a second language teachers.

Salaries improve from EFL teaching to the English medium schools as do the terms and conditions, often with extras such as housing, medical insurance and home flights being part of the employment package.

At university level there are a number of universities who instruct students through the medium of English and these recruit native English-speaking lecturers up to professor level. These are mostly in Istanbul and Ankara, but there is increasing demand from more universities to offer improved language skills as part of their degree programmes.

All teaching jobs require the teacher to have a degree in the subject they teach and a teaching qualification is generally required to teach in a school. For university lecturers a Master's degree, at least, is usually required before a lecturing job can be offered.

Consultancy

Other job prospects can be limited, unless you speak Turkish. However, management consultancy and advisory work is one area growing in

Istanbul and there are a number of companies specialising in working with international firms to help them do business in Turkey, or help Turkish firms develop business abroad. With market- or sector-specific skills that are in demand there will be less of a requirement to speak Turkish in these roles.

Tourism

Official and unofficial work in the tourist industry can sometimes be found in areas popular with foreign tourists and backpackers. The resort hotels catering to foreign package tours will often recruit their foreign staff from outside the country through their home country website, requiring advance planning to hit the pre-season recruitment timetable. Unofficial work found in Turkey will usually be low paid, or in exchange for food and accommodation.

WORK AND HOLIDAY PROGRAMME IN TURKEY FOR AUSTRALIANS

Australia has Work and Holiday (W&H) Programmes with a number of countries, including Turkey. The programmes allow young Australians to have an extended international holiday and supplement their travel funds with temporary or casual work.

The Turkish programme allows up to six months' work with each employer and study for up to four months. Young Australians between 18 and 30 years of age can stay in Turkey for up to 12 months from the date of entry. As with most of these programmes the opportunity can only be used once.

In addition to the standard documents required for a Turkish visa, this programme also requires:

- original certificate of police records (from the Australian federal police);
- proof of medical insurance for one year;

- a statutory declaration stating that that the applicant has no dependent children;
- original educational certificate or other evidence of successful completion of at least two years' undergraduate university study, issued by the institution attended;
- proof of sufficient funds to purchase a return airline ticket whilst in Turkey;
- letter of government support from the Department of Immigration and Citizenship.

The letter of support is issued by the Department of Immigration and Citizenship, ACT & Regions Office in Canberra, P.O.Box 717, Canberra City ACT 2601, or from 3 Lonsdale Street, Braddon ACT 2612.

FINDING EMPLOYMENT

Job vacancies are sometimes advertised in the English language papers (e.g. *Turkish Daily News*) published in Turkey, and people already living or working in the country may be head-hunted, or find out about a new job by word of mouth. However, most jobs for expatriates will be advertised outside the country through recruitment agencies or specialist publications.

The reason the vacancies are mainly advertised outside the country is that the preferred way to obtain a work permit requires an application to be made by the employer in Turkey and by the employee at a Turkish Embassy or Consulate abroad.

There is also the requirement that an employer must demonstrate that they cannot employ a local national to the job, which is usually done on the basis of demonstrating a need for mother tongue foreign language skills, linked to a degree and specialist qualification in a specific subject or skill.

Regional and sector opportunities

The North West

The majority of the industrialised part of the Turkish economy is based in the north west corner of the country, extending in a block from Ankara in the bottom right corner to Izmir in the bottom left, Istanbul in the top left corner and Zonguldak in the top right. The industries found here include food processing, textiles, construction, banking and finance, automotive manufacturing and white goods manufacturing.

Central Anatolia

The economy of central Anatolia is agriculture-based, producing huge quantities of corn, sugar beet and mutton. Large flour mills, with their tall silos, are often the only structure you can see when driving across the Anatolian plateau.

Ankara

Ankara, located deep in the heart of Anatolia, was chosen as the capital of the new Republic for its very remoteness, to make it less susceptible to attack by Greece and the European powers during the fragile early years of the new country. Though surrounded by the endless plateau, as the seat of government and the military it is a city of diplomats, soldiers, sailors and airmen, civil servants, industrialists supplying the government and academics from the numerous universities.

Mediterranean and Aegean Coasts

Around the Mediterranean and Aegean coasts there are many tourism- and property-based businesses. From small hotels and pensions to large resort hotels, along with self-catering apartments, villas and campsites there are endless accommodation options to complement the restaurants, bars and nightclubs of the region. These are matched by yacht charters, tour guides, water parks and all the facilities you would expect in a hot, seafront country that attracts millions of visitors every year from cooler, northern climes.

Izmir

In Izmir and the surrounding area there are a large number of trading companies, utilising the port facilities to export the food products of Anatolia and the citrus fruits of the coastal region that are processed nearby. Its attraction as a place to invest is highlighted by the fact that the large UK supermarket chain, Tesco, launched itself in the Turkish market by buying a small chain of shops based in Izmir.

Çeyhan

The south central city of Çeyhan is the terminal of the oil pipeline from Baku in Azerbaijan and the nearby port city of Mersin is the export hub for the whole eastern half of the country. Though neither are attractive cities in themselves, Mersin is considered one of the most relaxed cities in Turkey.

Cappadocia

Cappadocia, to the south east of Ankara, has become increasingly popular with foreigners looking to set up facilities for backpackers, who are the predominant visitors to the area, with Australians seeming to find it particularly attractive. With only a small numbers of visitors reaching Cappadocia, when compared to the Aegean and Mediterranean coasts, the big hotel operators have not been attracted to the area. As the independent travellers who do make it are usually looking for small boutique hotels, or low cost facilities, this makes it a great place for a small investor to break into the tourism market – unless you want to be by the sea.

Education sector

In the education sector there is strong demand for foreign staff, from TEFL teachers to university-level doctoral professors.

TEFL vacancies will be advertised by online specialist recruiters, in 'work abroad' magazines and by agencies in newspapers. Occasionally, the larger EFL schools in Turkey will advertise vacancies on their own website. A TEFL teacher will usually need to have at least a TEFL certificate to secure official employment, but is also likely to need a degree-level qualification.

Mainstream schools will advertise vacancies in newspapers such as the *Times Education Supplement* (www.tes.co.uk) in the UK and international school recruitment agencies such as Search Associates and Carny Sandoe. To teach in a school in Turkey it is essential to have a degree in the subject you wish to teach as well as a recognised teaching qualification.

PROSCRIBED EMPLOYMENT

While the employment market is generally open to foreign nationals when an employer can prove the need to recruit internationally, there are a number of professions where foreigners are specifically excluded from working.

The list of proscribed professions is quite wide and includes doctors, as well as bar singers and tour guides. The utilities network is also off limits to foreign workers as it is designated a national security area.

RECOGNITION OF HIGHER EDUCATION DIPLOMAS

Most countries require that some checks are done on a foreign national's educational qualifications prior to them taking up employment, especially as the foreign worker has usually been employed on the basis that the employer could not find a local national suitably qualified for the job.

In Turkey the equivalency procedure can take place after employment has started and is facilitated by the employer. To complete the process you need (where appropriate):

* the original or certified copy of the diploma;
* the original of the diploma or certificate of graduation presented for determination of equivalency;
* a complete transcript, indicating courses taken, grades received and credit hours, certified by a university;

- a notarised Turkish translation of any documents written in a foreign language;

- your passport.

The Equivalency Commission examines the documents submitted and passes a recommendation to the Executive Board of Higher Education, who generally ratify the recommendation of the Commission. The Board includes at least two recognised Turkish teachers, who can direct an investigation if required to gain clarification of the paperwork.

The concern of the Commission is to determine whether:

- the documents are authentic and unaltered;

- the documents relate to the applicant;

- the university or institution of higher education which awarded the diploma and the educational programme concerned is recognised in its own country;

- the level of the programme concerned is educationally equivalent to that offered at Turkish universities.

The commission can ask an applicant to demonstrate proof of their attendance at the institution and to supply any other information it requires to award the equivalency.

Submitting forged, or altered, documents is a criminal offence and the Commission and Board automatically notify the authorities to initiate a prosecution.

Upon successful completion of the procedure an equivalency certificate is issued to the applicant.

The process is managed by the Council of Higher Education for the Republic of Turkey (Türkiye Cumhurriyet Yükseköğretim Kurulu Başkanlığı – YÖK, 06539 Bilkent, Ankara; Tel +90 312 298 7000; Fax +90 312 266 4759; www.yok.gov.tr) and more information on the equivalency procedures can be found at: www.yok.gov.tr/english/index_en.htm.

WORK PERMITS

The detail on how to obtain a work permit is covered in Chapter 3, so is not covered here. Work Permits are obtained through the Ministry of Labour and Social Security (Çalışma ve Sosyal Güvenlik Bakanlığı, İnönü Bulvarı No 42, Emek, Ankara; Tel +90 312 296 6000; www.csgb. gov.tr; www.calisma.gov.tr; www.yabancicalismaizni.gov.tr/english/index_eng. htm) and issued by Ministry of Interior in Ankara.

A Work Permit is mandatory for foreign nationals and is best obtained from a Turkish Embassy before travelling to Turkey and must be requested by your future employer from within Turkey. However, it is possible to obtain a work permit after entering the country as long as you have a visitor's permit valid for at least six months. Further details for employers can be obtained from the Ministry of Labour and Social Security.

EMPLOYMENT LEGISLATION

Turkey follows the International Labour Organization (ILO) guidelines for employment, specifies a minimum wage, redundancy payments, maximum length working of the working day, the standard number of hours in a working week and has rules governing overtime. There is also specific legislation covering health and safety regulations.

Larger firms are also expected to employ a specific percentage of disabled staff as well as convicted criminals. Many firms, however, ignore this rule as any fines for non-compliance are relatively minor.

Unionisation is high and unions are active in collective bargaining arrangements. Unions demonstrate regularly. This has resulted in wages for urban workers being much higher than the minimum wage, especially for those with special skills and for professional staff. Salaries for highly-skilled professionals in Istanbul will often be not much different from those of similarly-qualified staff elsewhere in Europe.

SOCIAL INSURANCE

Using compulsory social insurance contributions, Turkey operates a nationwide public health and social security system. Foreign nationals who contribute to the system, and their families, are eligible to use the public hospitals and claim other benefits, including a pension, once they have reached the required threshold of payments.

The health system is wide-ranging and staffed with well-qualified professionals, though it does suffer from under-funding when compared to demand. It is not uncommon for doctors to speak at least one foreign language and to have undergone part of their training abroad. As in many public health systems around the world, senior doctors, consultants and specialists will often have a private practice where they offer their service to those willing and able to pay for better surroundings and to bypass the waiting lists. Most expats will be able to use these private services under the terms of their private medical insurance.

Contributions

Social insurance contributions are split between employee and employer at 14% and 19.5% respectively, while self-employed workers contribute 40% of their salary to the scheme. Historically there have been a number of separate schemes, e.g. private sector workers, civil servants and self-employed, but under pressure from the IMF to implement a more efficient system it is planned to combine the various schemes into one over-arching programme.

Foreign employees can elect to pay a reduced contribution if they agree to waive their right to claim disability and other benefits.

VOLUNTEERING IN TURKEY

For people not wanting to, or unable to, take up paid employment in Turkey, there is the option of volunteering. Volunteer jobs vary significantly in the need for skills and the length of time you are expected to commit to a particular project.

The options include, but are not limited to jobs in:

- agriculture,
- education,
- environment,
- archaeology,
- culture and local development,
- social support.

Some of the volunteer jobs in Turkey are in remote communities and it should be remembered that in central Anatolia the winters are very severe and most unlike winters on the Aegean and Mediterranean coasts. In some villages the accommodation can be basic and the home comforts may well be in short supply. Details of a number of voluntary organisations accepting international volunteers are listed in Appendix A.

7
Setting up a Business

INVESTING IN TURKEY

An alternative to finding employment in Turkey is to invest in an existing company, or to set up your own business.

As a member of the Organisation for Economic Co-operation and Development (OECD) and prospective member of the European Union, the investment environment in Turkey has improved dramatically over recent years and there is a well-trodden path for foreign investors to follow.

Legal matters

As in many other countries, the Turkish government has set up an agency (General Directorate of Foreign Investment) to encourage and facilitate inward investment. Changes to property law, tighter control of inflation and other measures implemented during the EU accession process and as a part of IMF sponsored economic measures have resulted in a climate attractive to foreign investors. In 2003 a new law on foreign direct investment was enacted to further protect the right of the investors and enhance the investment environment.

The new law gives equal rights to foreign and domestic companies, allows 100% foreign ownership of companies and gives foreign investors the right to choose any business structure allowed under Turkish law.

Foreign investors also have the right to purchase land and property, transfer profits freely and employ expatriate staff where necessary.

Business incentives

Large investors

For industrial investors there are a number of specialist development zones offering high-tech facilities and infrastructure and in some cases these are set up next to a university to further enhance the specialist support available. The zones are broadly split into technology development zones, organised industrial zones and special zones for large scale projects. There are approvals for 17 technology zones and close to 100 industrial zones, spread around the country. All of these zones are primarily intended for large scale investors.

For larger investors there are a number of incentive schemes covering VAT on the purchase of machinery and plant, customs duties on imported machinery and plant, accelerated depreciation and so on. To qualify for this scheme an investment of at least YTL200,000 is required in priority development areas and YTL400,000 elsewhere.

A wide range of sectors qualify for incentives under the above scheme and these include manufacturing, R & D, environmental protection, quality assurance, services and relocation of facilities from developed regions to priority areas. Additionally, investments in the agro-food industry and mining in priority development regions also attract incentives. Businesses must employ a minimum of 50 people within a set timescale for the incentives to apply.

Applications for the incentives should be submitted to any branch of certain designated banks who screen applications before passing them on the General Directorate of Incentives and Implementation, at the Undersecretariat of the Treasury. The designated banks are:

- Halkbank;
- Turkish Development Bank;
- Vakifbank;

- Ziraat Bank;
- Turkish Industrial Development Bank.

Small investors

Smaller investors also attract limited incentives, including customs exemptions, VAT exemptions on imported and domestically produced machinery and plant as well as subsidised financing. SMEs in Turkey are defined along international lines and businesses with up to 250 employees and a turnover of less than YTL250m fall into this category.

For an SME to qualify for the incentives, any investment must not exceed YTL950,000. To obtain the necessary incentive certificate an investor needs to apply to a branch of one of the following banks, who will, after initial evaluation and approval, submit the relevant documents to the Undersecretariat of the Treasury, who after a final successful evaluation will issue the incentive certificates:

- Turkish Development Bank for investments in the tourism, education, health and agro-industry sectors;
- Halkbank or Turkish Industrial Development Bank for all other sectors.

BUSINESS TYPES

There are four main types of business in Turkey suitable for foreign investors, while there is also the option for an individual to work as a sole trader.

Limited Liability Company

- Limited to between two and 50 shareholders.
- Requires a minimum of YTL5,000 capital.
- 25% of capital must be paid up.
- Shareholders make company decisions.

- LLCs are prohibited from operating in the banking and insurance sectors.

- Application for registration is made to the provincial trade registration office under the auspices of the local trade or industrial chamber.

Joint Stock Company

- Requires five or more shareholders.

- Requires a minimum of YTL50,000 capital.

- A board of at least three directors is required.

- Companies acting as banks require a board of at least five directors.

- Companies acting as banks require at least YTL30,000,000 capital.

- Application for registration is made to the Ministry of Industry and Trade (Sanayi ve Ticaret Bakanlığı) or the provincial trade registration office under the auspices of the local trade or industrial chamber.

Branch Offices

- A branch office operates as an extension of a foreign or domestic company, but must be registered with the authorities. Any branch office of a foreign company will be treated as non-resident for tax purposes.

- Application for registration is made to the Ministry of Industry and Trade or the provincial trade registration office under the auspices of the local trade or industrial chamber.

Liaison Offices

- Liaison offices require a permit to operate, which will only be given for a three year period in the first instance. Three year extensions can be applied for and the previous activities of the office will be taken into consideration. A liaison office cannot carry out any commercial activity.

- Application for registration is made to the Under-secretariat of the Treasury.

Sole Trader: Proprietor (*Mal sahibi*) or Artisan (*Esnaf*)

- Depending on the type of business undertaken the designation of a sole trader will vary as above. In both cases the individual has unlimited liability if their business fails, as does any partnership that two or more individuals may form.

- Application for registration is made to the Trade Registry Office of the Ministry of Industry and Trade.

- Registration with the tax authorities (Treasury Ministry – Başbakanlık Hazine Müsteşarlığı) to obtain a tax code is also required.

Whilst the process of setting up a company is straightforward and quick when compared to many countries, it can be easier employing a company formation agent to do the running around, make introductions and translate at crucial points along the way. The Turkish British Chamber of Commerce and Industry (Bury House, 33 Bury Street, London SW1Y 6AU; Tel +44 20 7321 0999; www.tbcci.org) maintains a list of such agents on its website.

TRADE LICENCES

There is no requirement for trade licences in Turkey, but approval is needed from the Treasury to set up a company working in the financial sector, which includes insurance, trade finance, leasing and foreign exchange.

TOURISM BUSINESS SPECIFICS

The Turkish government promotes tourism development within the country and advertises extensively around the world. In recent years there has been a drive to tighten up control of the industry and reduce unplanned and illegal developments. In some cases demolition of unlicensed development has been ordered by the courts. Eco-tourism, adventure tourism, special interest tourism, independent travel and sailing have been promoted in recent years as demand for all-inclusive package holidays in big hotels has lost some of its appeal.

For independent business people, a tourism-related business can be particularly attractive in Turkey as it offers a great lifestyle, in a wonderful place, with lower overheads and start-up costs than elsewhere in Europe. This is especially true of the cost of property required for the business.

Five countries (Germany, UK, Russian Federation, Bulgaria and Holland) account for more than 50% of tourist arrivals and it is not uncommon for a tourist business to specialise in providing services for a particular nationality.

A tourism project can only be built on land designated for such activity on the local plan (*imar plani*) and a tourism development on land designated for other purposes runs the risk of being demolished. If an area has not been included in an *imar plani* at all, an application can be made to designate the land as a tourism development area.

To acquire government land for development of a tourism business requires an application to be made to the Ministry of Tourism and Culture. A business plan, proof of funding and demonstration of expertise in the sector will be required, along with the relevant application forms.

When setting up any tourism enterprise a Tourism Operation Permit is required before moving from the development stage and commencing trading activities in the sector.

The Ministry of Tourism and Culture regulates and supervises the tourism sector, however, the General Directorate of Investments and Enterprises of the ministry oversees investment transactions and projects.

Potential investors can also contact the Tourism and Cultural Counsellor at their nearest Turkish Embassy or Consulate.

ACCOUNTING

Businesses are required by law to keep accurate accounts, have them audited and submit annual tax returns. The auditing requirement is rarely applied, though the protection of an audit may be worth the cost for company directors.

Service providers offering services to foreign-owned businesses often register with the international business organisations (e.g. British Chamber of Commerce in Turkey, Turkish US Business Council) and foreign embassies in Turkey who may place the lists on their websites or distribute the information to their members or nationals.

LABOUR MARKET

There is a large labour market in Turkey, with over 24 million people (34% of the population) of working age. Unemployment is high, at around 10%, giving a good supply of labour for expanding companies.

Manufacturing employs approximately 19% of the workforce, trade and tourism 20% and agriculture and fishing 30%.

A minimum wage is set by the government, but though actual wages are higher than this, they are usually well below northern European levels. Salaries are offered gross, with tax and national insurance contributions deducted at source.

Social security contributions are high compared to North America, but comparable to much of Europe with employers' contributions standing at around 25% and employees contributions at 15%.

Employment benefits

With high unionisation and strong collective bargaining many workers have valuable fringe benefits including meals, works transportation and significant annual bonuses. Social benefits may also be paid for: births, marriages, deaths, heating and clothing allowances are paid in some areas.

The comprehensive and free education system has resulted in a highly-skilled workforce and Turkey ranks well in the world for the availability of skilled workers and managers. Strong foreign language provision in schools and large numbers of tourists also means there are many multi-lingual staff in the labour market.

Officially the working week is 45 hours and there is a maximum of 270 hours overtime allowed in any one year.

Paid holiday becomes an entitlement after one year of employment and the level increases from 14 days per year in the first five years to 26 days after 15 years.

Women are entitled to paid maternity leave of 16 weeks, split as eight weeks before the expected delivery date and eight weeks after the actual delivery date.

Notice of termination of employment varies from two weeks for employment lasting less than six months to eight weeks for employment lasting over three years. Redundancy payments of 30 days for each full year worked are due, and based on gross salary, including all fringe benefits.

ECONOMIC SUMMARY

Economic indicators are good, with a population of over 70 million and a GDP of $360bn, Turkey is in the top 20 economies of the world and the top ten in Europe. Growth rates are the envy of many countries, with figures of up to 10% per annum in recent years.

Agriculture

Agriculture is a declining contributor to GDP, with manufacturing and the service sector growing. The customs union with the EU, which came into force in 1996, covers manufactured and processed agricultural products, but not raw agricultural products. The effect is that Turkey has become a manufacturing base for many companies looking to take advantage of lower costs without having to face import tariffs when manufactured products enter Europe.

Industry

The automotive sector is particularly well established in Turkey, with Renault, Fiat, Toyota, Hyundai, Honda, Isuzu, BMC, M.A.N., Mercedes-Benz and Ford all having a presence alongside Turkish competitors. A total of more than 900,000 vehicles was produced in Turkey in 2005, generating close to US$8 billion of export revenue.

To complement the automotive industry is a well-developed components sector employing 70,000 people in almost 30,000 companies with more that 2,400 companies exporting to Europe, Africa, the Russian Federation, the Middle East and Central Asia.

Turkey is one of the leading manufacturers worldwide in the production of white goods. Approximately ten million units of washing machines, dishwashers and refrigerators are produced annually for the domestic and export markets.

Carpets and Textiles

Turkey is famous for carpet production, but the textile and clothing sector are equally important though less well known to those outside the trade. The country is a leading producer of organic cotton, that complements its wool production which includes more than the native Angora wool. In addition to supplying yarn to other manufacturing countries (Italy is a major buyer of Turkish cotton), Turkey supplies leading fashion houses around the world with designer clothes, as well as non-branded items for the high-street market.

Other fashion items that are produced in large numbers include shoes, jewellery and leather goods. Europe and the Russian Federation are major export markets for these goods, with jewellery also going to the Middle East and North America.

Ceramics and Glass

Ceramic production has been a long-standing tradition in the region, with producers extending from Turkey through to Iran. In Turkey the industry has developed a long way from the production of decorative tiles and glazed brickwork, though beautiful items in these forms are still produced. Iznik and Kütahya are the centre of the industry, producing modern tiles, sanitary-ware and kitchenware and are world leaders in the sector.

The glass industry is also long-standing and Turkish companies work with all areas of the industry from household glass production to the glass reinforced plastic sector and complement their manufacturing experience with in-house design and research facilities.

Furniture

Furniture production is extensive, but mostly on a small scale with an average of three employees per manufacturer.

The furniture district in Istanbul is well known for producing hand carved wooden furniture, while the Siteler district in Ankara is home to over 10,000 small businesses involved in producing classical and modern handmade furniture. The small firms are complemented by a handful of larger companies with mass-production facilities making Turkey the second largest exporter of sofa beds in the world.

Tourism

Tourism has played a key role in developing the Turkish economy by bringing in foreign currency and making the country more cosmopolitan. With wonderful weather along the 8,000 kilometres of coastline, beautiful scenery, dramatic mountains, winter and summer tourist activities and historical sites to rival any country in the world, it is no wonder that 22 million people visit the country or sail along its coastline every year.

REASONS TO INVEST IN TURKEY

There are many reasons for Turkey's attractiveness to foreign investors, both large scale and on a smaller more personal level. The Turkish inward investment organisation lists a number of commercial reasons for investing in Turkey as shown below, but for many people the attraction of Turkey is as much its culture, climate and scenery as the excellent business environment.

Top Ten Official Reasons to Invest in Turkey

- Proximity to Europe, Central Asia and the Middle East.
- Excellent environment for foreign investment (15,000 foreign investment projects).
- Strong economic growth expected to be above 5% per annum for the next five to ten years.
- Large domestic market of 73 million people with a growing GNP.
- Highly skilled workforce.
- High quality standards and programmes.
- Good sources of energy from Central Asia and the Middle East.
- Modern telecommunications network.
- Strong political links with Central Asia and the Caucasus.
- Low cost base, when compared to Europe.

8
Retiring to Turkey

DECIDING TO RETIRE ABROAD

Retiring abroad to a sunny climate, with a home on the beach and a life away from the cares of working life is a dream for many. Great holidays, TV programmes and the stories of friends have all inspired people to retire abroad, but the reality of living somewhere for twelve months of the year is a very different proposition to one week on an all-inclusive package tour.

Despite its reputation as a hot country with endless sunshine and a great outdoor lifestyle, Turkey can get damp and chilly in winter along the coasts and bitterly cold inland. From the beaches of the popular summer holiday resort of Antalya you can even see snow on the hills in winter.

Some of the seaside towns, whilst bustling and lively in the summer, become almost ghost towns in the winter, with many of the Turkish shopkeepers returning to their villages for the closed season. Restaurants, shops and services can all but disappear, as will all the fresh fruit and vegetables, which are still very much seasonal in Turkey without the large supermarkets flying in food from all over the world. The number of foreign residents also drops in winter, with many apartments being used only for summer holidays or short breaks.

Some towns and villages have attracted larger numbers of expatriate retirees and these can be a good choice for many as there will be other residents nearby who share a common language and cultural background. Having someone to share your international experience with is something that many people find an essential part of making life abroad enjoyable. Careful research will also show that different villages have attracted different nationalities of retirees. Though a broad generalisation, German retirees seem to have tended to congregate east of Antalya, whilst the British retirees have spread westwards along the Mediterranean and northwards up the Aegean coast.

Keeping Active

Depending on what you wish to do to keep yourself occupied, certain parts of the country may be more appealing than others. Golf, for example, has become a major attraction at Belek, near Antalya, with a number of championship quality courses offering attractively priced playing opportunities. Some areas, such as Izmir, have lots of historical and religious attractions, while others have sailing, hiking and outdoor activities.

A more temperate climate than the heat of the Mediterranean summer may be appealing for gardeners, unless you wish to grow plants suited to the local conditions. Knowing what lifestyle you are seeking will help guide you to a decision on whether Turkey is the right place for you, and if so, where in the country you should look for somewhere to live.

Accessibility

Flights to Europe also stop from many of the regional airports in winter, as few of the flights are scheduled operations, but rather charter flights to serve the package tour operators. What can be a straightforward flight from a regional UK airport to the southern coast of Turkey in summer can turn into a long day of travelling to distant airports, or multiple flights if you fly from a regional airport to an international hub and then onward to the final destination.

For some people all this can be a positive benefit and part of the reason they want to live abroad. For others it can become a problem as they miss family and friends at home and find the long winters are not quite what they were expecting.

Trial run

Before making the decision to sell up everything in your home country and buy a new home in Turkey, it could well be worth spending a winter in rented accommodation in your chosen destination to experience at first hand the changing seasons of Turkey. It is much easier to change your mind after a winter in rented accommodation than after going through the buying process and owning your own home, especially as second hand homes are often more difficult to sell than new ones.

CHOOSING YOUR RETIREMENT HOME

Choosing a retirement home presents its own challenges.

With a retirement home the decision needs to be as much about how you will be living in the future, as about life next week. With retirement and life in your autumnal years comes the consequences of ageing. Hills, steps and staircases all become more of a challenge in later years. The distance to local shops which, when you can drive is of no concern, can be a different matter when you need to rely on public transport.

Apart from your ability to get around your home, as well as to and from friends, neighbours and amenities, another major consideration is maintaining the property. The fabric of the building, as well as the décor and the outside areas will all need work. The climate of Turkey has its own effect on buildings and gardens and activities that can be a pleasure could easily turn into frustrating chores, or require expensive outside help to complete.

For couples, your own company may be all you need, but if the health of one partner declines, or one of you is widowed, then some places can be lonely and devoid of company of people from your own culture. Most people require a social network of some sort and making sure there will be suitable opportunities to make the friends you need, both now and in the future, should be a priority before buying a property rather than after.

Proximity to health services and a doctor who speaks your language should also be considered. Advancing age often requires increased use of healthcare services and travelling long distances in times of need or pain is not to be recommended. The Turkish healthcare system is very different from that in the UK and elsewhere in Europe, with families taking much more responsibility for ageing relatives and the state providing a lot less input. Without your own family close by, private arrangements might be necessary to ensure that you have adequate support and assistance for your daily needs.

Your choice of home, therefore, should be carefully considered. You may fall in love with a magnificently-placed, cliff-top house, at the end of winding track, down 20 steps and overlooking the sea, but in a few years' time negotiating the steps, let alone carrying all the shopping to it, may be beyond you.

An isolated house on the edge of a traditional Turkish village may seem idyllic, but unless you can learn Turkish reasonably quickly and are happy with only local friends, it can become quite lonely.

Finally, always approach buying a home abroad in the same way as you would in your home country – with caution. If a deal seems to good to be true, it probably is.

Always use your own lawyer experienced in Turkish property matters, preferably one recommended by your Embassy, not the property agent or the seller. And always follow the correct procedures. There are plenty of rogue builders and property agents waiting to part you from your money, just like everywhere else in the world.

PRIME RETIREMENT LOCATIONS

The favourite places to retire to in Turkey are different from the places most expatriates go to for work. Ankara, Istanbul and Izmir are the prime work locations, but the Aegean and Mediterranean coasts are the prime retirement hotspots.

Having only recently opened up its property market to foreigners, and mortgages being new products on the Turkish financial market, there are far fewer retirees in Turkey than there are in Spain. Fewer than 100,000 foreigners own property in Turkey, whereas 600,000 Britons alone own property in Spain.

An estimated 34,000 Britons live in Turkey, with around 1,000 being formally retired (i.e. 65 or 60 for men and women respectively).

With fewer expatriate retirees than in Spain, Turkish culture still holds sway in all the areas popular with foreign retirees and, for many, this is the appeal of the place. Germans, French, Dutch, Britons and Americans are the leading foreign property buyers in Turkey, with Australians seemingly concentrating, in small numbers, in buying tourism businesses in Cappadocia and the Dardanelles.

Due to its large size and diverse nature there are lots of options in terms of type, size and location of property in Turkey. Working out what you want, what services you need and where you want to buy before starting your property hunt will help ensure you do not get sidetracked by estate agents or a particularly spectacular view.

The main tourist areas are also the prime retirement areas, which broadly speaking stretch from Çeşme, on the Aegean, to Side on the Mediterranean. Different areas have attracted different nationalities and the local airports are often served by different airlines that fly to limited destinations reflecting the nationality of the majority of tourists and retirees.

PROPERTY TYPES

It is not many years since the coastal villages of Turkey were small, isolated and dependent on fishing. Twenty years of booming tourism has seen numerous building projects that now dominate the skyline and, as Turkey is also in an active earthquake zone, there is a distinct lack of old buildings in some areas.

Traditionally, Turkish houses have looked uncared-for externally. However, as the economy has boomed over the past decade there is more money being spent on buildings and with the liberalisation of the property market more homes are being built with foreign buyers in mind. The result is an increasing number of buildings that are built in the aesthetically-pleasing Mediterranean style. At the same time gardens are becoming increasingly common.

Whether you are looking for an apartment, villa, village house, building plot, new build or established property, they are all available in Turkey, though not always in all areas. From old Ottoman houses in Bursa to underground cave houses in Cappadocia, there is also a variety of uniquely Turkish houses for the adventurous or eccentric buyer.

FINANCIAL BUDGETING

Retiring abroad for a perceived lower cost of living is a common idea. Turkey can appear to be the ideal choice, with low property prices, warm weather to reduce heating bills and bountiful fresh fruit and vegetables at budget prices in summer markets.

Property is indeed cheaper, and property taxes reasonable, which can be a good start in lowering your costs. If you are fortunate enough to be able to sell a property in your home country and buy for much less in Turkey the remainder can be a nice nest egg to fund your retirement. However, if you ever need to move back to your home country then it can be a real struggle to afford to do so.

The warm climate can seem appealing if you have spent your life in northern and central Europe, but one of the problems of living somewhere warm like Mediterranean Turkey is that you get used to the summer heat and when the winter drop in temperature comes along, the change can be as great as, or greater than back home. Turkish homes are often not well insulated, making then feel damp and chilly in winter, and without central heating the cost of using electric heaters can mount up.

Being mostly self-sufficient in food, and exporting a lot of agricultural produce to Europe, the shops' supply of fruit and vegetables can be highly seasonal. At certain times of the year there is plenty of cheap fruit and salad, but at others there can be a dearth of anything other than carrots and potatoes. Eating a local diet, low in meat and high in carbohydrates, can easily be done on a budget and sometimes it can seem to be cheaper to eat out in local cafés than to eat at home, but if you prefer to eat your own traditional meals then the costs can mount up quickly.

Retirees do not qualify for the state healthcare system, so purchasing medical insurance becomes a necessity if you want to ensure you can access medical attention promptly in time of need. Unless you need emergency lifesaving medical help then you will be asked how you intend to pay before you are treated at a hospital or medical centre.

While state hospitals are served by professional and well trained staff, the facilities are not what many Europeans and North Americans would be used to and so the majority of foreigners use the private healthcare system to avoid the queues and enjoy pleasanter surroundings.

The upshot is, that if you want to live your current lifestyle and eat your favourite foods from home, then living in Turkey is not necessarily cheaper. Careful planning and budgeting will help determine whether or not Turkey is the right choice for you, which for many people it is and will continue to be so for many more years in the future.

ENJOYING YOUR RETIREMENT

A move to a new place for, or during, your retirement will usually mean that you have to create a whole new social network and find new ways to continue your hobbies, enjoy favourite pastimes and, in the case of living abroad, source books, DVDs and other material in your native language.

Making new friends can take a while, but with some time and effort there will be plenty of people to meet, and if you manage to learn Turkish to some extent then there will be many more people with whom to socialise.

Using the internet to identify expatriate groups and newsletters for international retirees in general, as well as those in Turkey, can help speed up the process of meeting people. This can also help with identifying like-minded people with whom to enjoy activities and trips.

Some of the main expat sites for Turkey are listed in Appendix A, but there are many others that will also be useful.

Historic sites

Turkey is blessed with many historic sites and joining guided tours, or simply visiting places with someone knowledgeable about the particular site, can greatly enhance the pleasure of a visit, as well as providing the opportunity to meet new people.

Gardening

Gardening is a popular hobby for many retired people, but the climate will mean a change in technique and it will be well worth planning ahead and buying a book on growing Mediterranean plants as well as gardening in a water-poor region. Seeds can be easily taken with you, but plants are more difficult to transport and generally need a phyto-sanitary health certificate from your local Government Agriculture Department before you can transport them internationally.

Hobbies

Other hobbies such as painting, photography, writing, sailing and craftwork are also easily continued in Turkey. With the help of internet shopping and an international subscription to a favourite magazine your chosen hobby can be as easily enjoyed abroad as in your home country.

With all hobbies, some planning before you move will help greatly in being able to continue the hobby. You will find it useful to secure a supply of materials and identify required support and information on developing your skills before you leave, as this is more easily done in your own language, or when resources are available on a newsagent's shelf nearby.

With the advent of the internet, continuing education is easily accessible anywhere in the world. More traditional correspondence courses are still available, but many are now delivered online, or via email. Whether you want to learn a new skill for a hobby or a profession, or follow a formal course and gain a certificate you always regretted not getting at school, there are many options, some of which are listed in Appendix A.

SOCIAL SECURITY AND PENSIONS

British Retirees

If you are eligible for a UK state pension when you retire, you will still be able claim it if you retire abroad. However, you will only receive the index-linked annual increases if you live in the European Economic Area (EEA), Switzerland, or another country with which the UK has social security and pensions agreement. Turkey is included among such countries with agreements on social security and pensions and a UK state pension can be paid directly into a UK or Turkish bank account. If weekly payments are under £5 then one annual payment will made instead.

For people who want to divide their time between two countries you need to decide where to receive your payment, as only one bank account can be nominated.

Taxation

For tax purposes, UK pensions are taxable income, but if they are received by someone living in Turkey they are only taxable in Turkey. However, income derived from letting property in the UK may still be taxable in the UK, as may any capital gains made in the UK whilst resident in Turkey.

Health

There is no agreement between Turkey and the UK covering provision of medical services for nationals of each country living in the other. Therefore, as a British passport holder who is retired and living in Turkey you will not be eligible to use the Turkish health service free of charge.

Allowances and Benefits

There are a number of other UK benefits that retirees may be claiming before retiring abroad, including incapacity benefit, benefits for industrial diseases and injuries, widow's and bereavement benefit and guardian's benefit. In certain circumstances these can still be claimed when resident in Turkey. Early discussion with the Department for Work and Pensions will help with arranging continuity of benefits once you relocate to Turkey.

Only retirees living in the EEA are eligible for the winter fuel payment and, therefore, retirement to Turkey precludes receipt of this allowance.

Further information on payment of the above benefits whilst living in Turkey can be obtained from: Department for Work and Pensions, The Pension Service, International Pensions centre, Tyneview Park, Newcastle Upon Tyne NE98 1BA; Tel +44 191 218 777; Fax +44 191 218 3836; www.dwp.gov.uk.

For specific information on guardian's allowance contact HM Revenue and Customs, Child Benefit Office, P.O.Box 1, Washington, Newcastle Upon Tyne NE88 1AA; Tel +44 191 225 1536; Fax +44 191 225 1543; child.benefit@hmrc.gsi.gov.uk.

Rules covering private pension plans and the payment of benefits vary and the provider should be contacted directly to determine the implications of moving to Turkey.

Canadian Retirees

Canadian residents qualify for an old age security payment after living in Canada for ten years once they have reached the age of 18. However, the pension can only be collected outside of Canada if the retiree has lived in Canada for at least 20 years after reaching the age of 18.

Contributions of between three and ten years to the Canada pension plan may also qualify the contributor for a disability pension, and the members of their family may qualify for survivor or child benefits. The actual benefit entitlements depend on the age of the contributor and the type of benefit sought.

For both the old age security payment and the Canada pension plan, any pension for a qualifying resident will be based on the length of residence or the contributions made whilst living in Canada.

Further information can be obtained from: International Operations, Service Canada, Ottawa, Ontario K1A 0L4; Tel +1 613 957 1954; Fax +1 613 952-8901; from Canada or the United States (in English) 1 800 454-8731 or TDD 1 800 255-4786; www.servicecanada.gc.ca.

Rules covering private pension plans and the payment of benefits vary and the provider should be contacted directly to determine the implications of moving to Turkey.

Australian Retirees

An Australian pension can only be claimed by someone resident in Australia, or one of 18 countries with which Australia has an international social security agreement. At this time Australia has no agreement with Turkey and so an Australian state pension could not be claimed by someone living in Turkey.

Further information can be obtained from Centrelink International Services, GPO Box 273, Hobart TAS 7001, Australia; Tel 13 1673 inside Australia; Tel 00 800 6190 5703 freephone from Turkey; Tel +61 3 6222 3455 any international call; Fax +61 3 6222 2799; www.centrelink. gov.au; international.services@centrelink.gov.au.

Rules covering private pension plans and the payment of benefits vary and the provider should be contacted directly to determine the implications of moving to Turkey.

Kiwi Retirees

Depending on where you live outside of New Zealand there are a number of different systems in place governing payment of the state pension. If you are already receiving a New Zealand superannuation or veteran pension you can continue to claim it if you move abroad, but the amount payable depends on where you move to.

War disablement pensions, surviving spouse's pension, clothing allowance, gallantry award and funeral grant will still be paid wherever you go and are not affected by the country you choose.

The amount of New Zealand superannuation pension and the veteran's pension paid depends on where you live. If you move to Turkey you will be eligible to apply for 50% if you qualify in your own right for the pension, are a New Zealand resident, are currently living in New Zealand

and intend to live abroad for 26 weeks or more. It is also important to remember you cannot claim the living alone rate if you go overseas for longer than 30 weeks.

Payments will be made fortnightly to a New Zealand bank account or every four weeks to an account abroad. An application to take your pension abroad must be made at least four to six weeks before you leave New Zealand by calling New Zealand Superannuation (Tel 0800 552002 in New Zealand) to make an appointment. As well as a completed application form, you will need to show your own and your partner's passport, a second form of identification and travel itinerary or tickets at the subsequent meeting with New Zealand Superannuation.

Tax on your pension will be paid locally in Turkey and full payment of your pension will resumed if you return to live in New Zealand and notify the relevant authorities.

If you need assistance with any matter relating to your pension whilst living overseas you can contact International Services, Work and Income, P.O.Box 27178, Wellington, New Zealand; Tel +64 4 978 1180; Fax +64 4 918 0159; international-services@msd.govt.nz.

For assistance with a veteran's pension contact War Pension Services, P.O.Box 9448, Hamilton, New Zealand; Free Phone 0800 553 003; Free Fax 0508 402 402; warpension@msd.govt.nz.

Rules covering private pension plans and the payment of benefits vary and the provider should be contacted directly to determine the implications of moving to Turkey.

American Retirees

To qualify for a US federal pension you need to have worked for ten years in the USA. A pension can still be claimed if you live outside the USA, but it is not always possible for the payment to be made in the country where you live.

Further details can be obtained from your nearest US Social Security Office, the nearest US Embassy, or by writing to the Social Security

Administration, P.O. Box 17769, Baltimore, Maryland 21235-7769, USA; www.socialsecurity.gov.

Pensions for public sector workers outside of the federal system are usually administered by the individual state where the service is operated. Information on each state pension scheme and its procedures are included on the official website of the state concerned. Links to the websites of each state can be found at www.usa.gov/Agencies/State_and_Territories.shtml/.

Rules covering private pension plans and the payment of benefits vary and the provider should be contacted directly to determine the implications of moving to Turkey. Information and advice on your private pension rights can be obtained from the Consumer Rights Organization (www. pensionrights.org) that promotes and protects private pension rights in the USA.

RETIREMENT-SPECIFIC HEALTH ISSUES

In later years it is common for health issues to become increasingly intrusive. Sometimes problems come on slowly, other times they come on more suddenly. When living abroad it is important to plan for when health issues begin to affect your daily life.

Maintaining a healthy lifestyle will improve the likelihood of staying fitter for longer. Limiting alcohol intake, not smoking, taking moderate exercise and staying active mentally can all help stave off the effects of ageing.

Keeping an eye on your blood pressure and blood sugar levels, as well as relaxing and enjoying yourself are important too.

Common problem areas to consider include the cardiovascular system, eyesight, hearing, digestive and mobility issues. Alzheimers is a serious issue to deal with if it occurs and it can become a major problem for a partner to cope with the effects when they could well be able to continue living comfortably themselves.

Consulting your doctor before deciding to move abroad is advisable. Your doctor will be able to give you professional advice on staying healthy as well as making sure you are fit enough for the challenge of living abroad.

When living abroad without immediate family nearby and with less access to care facilities as they exist in your home country, it will be necessary to make private arrangements for help around the home, or for longer-term care in a nursing home should the need arise. This can be expensive and should be taken into account when working out your finances.

The implication of one partner dying before the other, especially the one least expected to pass away first, should also be considered.

Having made a home abroad it can often mean that you restrict your ability to move back into your home country's health care system. Most countries have a mandatory residency period that it is necessary to fulfil before you can access medical and nursing care. There have been a number of cases reported where people who have retired abroad have needed long-term care, but have been unable to afford it in their destination country and unable to return home as they no longer qualify for the service in their 'home' country.

Private health insurance may not cover you when living abroad, or you may need to pay an additional premium to ensure continued cover. Always notify your insurance company before moving and ask for information and advice when considering a move in the first instance.

Always consult the relevant authorities in your home country before moving abroad so you are fully informed of your rights and the implications of your move.

9
Finances

Managing your finances is always an ongoing, as well as essential, task. When all your income is from one source, and is deposited in one nearby bank, in one currency, if something goes wrong it is usually a relatively easy task to contact your bank and begin to sort out the problem. However, when living abroad and your money is in multiple currencies, in more than one country and your bank is either in a different country, or the bank staff all speak Turkish, then sorting out a problem becomes more challenging. There are other issues to consider too.

How you access your money, keeping it somewhere safe and accessible for when you really need it will not be so straightforward when you are likely to be spending a significant amount of time travelling internationally, or splitting your time between two countries. Advance planning of your likely timetable and how you will cost-effectively ensure you have good access to your money will reduce stress and bank charges.

Reliable access to emergency funds should also be considered. When living in a country where the social support system is not set up to look after the needs of foreigners, then you may need to be able personally to guarantee payment for emergency medical treatment until the insurance company confirms they will cover it. A family crisis in your home country may require you to purchase a plane ticket at very short notice, with a consequential high cost.

When living abroad many aspects of financial management you have taken for granted may well be different, and considering these before you move can reduce the likelihood of future problems. Modifying existing financial arrangements before you move can often be much more straightforward than doing so later.

BANKING

In Your Home Country

Whatever your arrangements in your home country, the minimum you should do is notify your financial institutions that you are moving abroad. Many companies will be happy to send all correspondence to you wherever you are so that they can retain your business, or you may be able to access everything you need on the internet.

However, where there are restrictions or restrictive terms and conditions on the specific services that the bank provides to you, you may well have to make some changes, or accept some changes imposed upon you by the bank.

For example, your current account may require you to pay in a minimum amount of money every month to qualify for reduced fees, or additional benefits. If you will no longer be paying your salary or pension into the account it may well become expensive to maintain and you would be better off changing the type of account you have with the bank.

There may also be a residency requirement for an account or service and if you are out of the country the facility may be frozen, or cancelled. Insurances can be one such item, especially where they are provided as an additional benefit on a bank account.

One benefit of moving abroad though, can sometimes be that any interest on a balance maintained at the bank is paid tax free. The bank will usually require a declaration of non-residency to be signed for this to happen and the implications of such a declaration should be considered before signing it – there can be implications on your future eligibility for state healthcare, pension and other commercial benefits.

An advantage to maintaining a bank account in your home country is that when you return for visits you will have easy access to funds. Additionally, if you are given cheques or cash for presents, you will have somewhere to deposit them easily and cheaply.

Where you need, or want, to continue with other financial commitments in your home country, a bank account there can also make this easier to do. Maintaining your pension plan, continuing with a savings plan, paying a mortgage or receiving revenue from rented property or other sources are all made easier and cheaper, by using a bank account in the country where the transactions are taking place.

A bank account in your home country can also be a good way of demonstrating that you have maintained close links with the country during your time abroad. This can be useful if you ever have to return because of illness, redundancy or other difficulty and you need to slot back into your country's social welfare system or health service.

In Turkey

For day-to-day living, using a Turkish bank account will be easier and cheaper than drawing funds on a bank account outside the country. The Turkish banking system has consolidated in recent years and the government has tightened up on the management of the banks to ensure their stability and improve their international reputation.

One of the key monitors of the consumer banking section is the Credit Reference Agency (Kredi Kayit Bürosu: www.kkb.com.tr) that the banks use to monitor and share credit reference information relating to private clients.

The Turkish banks are overseen by the Banking Regulation and Supervision Agency (Banlacilik Düzenleme ve Denetleme Kurumu: www.bddk.org.tr), which has extensive information about the Turkish banking system, in English, on its website.

To limit the opportunity for financial disputes and tighten up on the underground economy in Turkey, the government introduced a legal requirement that any transaction exceeding YTL8,000 must be carried out via a bank, financial institution or the post office (PTT).

Opening a bank account in Turkey is straightforward, though faci...
you can find a branch where the manager speaks your language. Turkish
banks generally provide free current accounts, though they will be non-
interest bearing. Charges become applicable for overdrafts and other
additional services.

You will need a Turkish tax number and to provide a copy of your passport
when applying to open an account at a branch in Turkey. You can apply to
an overseas office of a bank operating in Turkey to open an account before
you move to the country. You can also assign someone else to open an
account in Turkey on your behalf.

Single beneficiary accounts, as well as joint accounts are available and
you can decide at the point of opening the account whether a joint account
requires single or joint signatures to withdraw funds. You will be able to
open a standard current (cheque) account, as well as a savings account.
Turkish Lira and foreign currency denominated accounts are available.

Only the account holder(s) or signatory(ies) can authorise a withdrawal
of funds and a court order is required before details of the account can be
released to a third party.

There are both state-owned and private Turkish banks, as well as a number
of foreign banks. Individual branches are dotted around the country and,
whilst they offer broadly similar services, some will be more conveniently
located than others. Many of the banks listed in Appendix A have sections
of their website in English where details of their services are listed, as well
as the contact details of their international branches and representative
offices.

While most of the banks have English language sections and are promoting
their services to foreign residents, four banks (Türkiye Iş Bankasi, Türk
Ekonomi Bankasi, Türkiye Garanti and Millennium Bank) list specialist
expatriate services on their websites, along with the contact details of
branches specialising in offering these services.

Retail banking services offered by most banks in Turkey include:

• deposit accounts (YTL and foreign currency);

- current accounts (YTL and foreign currency);
- time deposits (TRY / foreign currency);
- debit cards;
- mutual funds;
- automated bill payments;
- overdraft facilities;
- cashpoint (ATM) card;
- telephone banking;
- internet banking;
- safety deposit boxes.

CREDIT CARDS

Credit cards have only become common in Turkey in the past ten years and the availability of credit is still restricted, when compared to the UK and US. However, the process of applying for Turkish credit cards is straightforward and if you already have a bank account with a bank it is also possible to apply online.

Cards backed by the internationally-recognised VISA and Mastercard are available, as is the well-known American Express card. Interest rates can be high, with monthly rates of over 4.5% charged by some banks on outstanding balances.

MORTGAGES

Mortgages are another recent introduction to the Turkish financial markets and have contributed to the rise in property prices. Though mortgages are a recent innovation, they are now widely offered by the banks. As the market is still developing, the structure of mortgages offered by the various institutions varies considerably.

Depending on the bank concerned, the term of any mortgage offered can vary from ten to 30 years. The loan to value (LTV) percentage can be as low as 50% and rarely goes above 80%. Mortgages are available in YTL as well as a variety of international currencies such as US$, GB£ and Euros with interest rates varying depending on the currency of the loan. Not all banks require the mortgage holder to be resident in Turkey, though the property must be if the borrower is based outside the country.

Other restrictions, limitations or conditions that apply on some mortgages vary significantly depending on the lender and some that are worth looking out for are listed below:

- available only on completed homes with a building certificate;
- available only on properties less than 20 years old;
- extended without the condition of being a Turkish resident;
- applicant must be 18 years old or over;
- buildings insurance is mandatory;
- life insurance on the mortgage holder is mandatory;
- the mortgage will be secured against the property.

As with opening a bank account, certain documentation is required to secure a mortgage:

- original and copy of your passport;
- payslip or statement of salary from your employer;
- copy of the title deed, or the building certificate for the property;
- Turkish tax identity card;
- proof of residential address by presentation of an original or copy of a recent electricity or telephone bill.

The cost of securing a mortgage can be significant, as can the mandatory insurances demanded by the mortgage lender. Some of the fees and additional costs are:

- an up-front fee of up to 2% of the value of the mortgage;
- a valuation fee of up YTL1,000 depending on the size of the property;

- life insurance;

- building insurance;

- earthquake insurance (DASK), which is compulsory for any property. The premium will vary depending on the size, location, age and construction of the property.

INSURANCE

There is a well-developed insurance (*sigorta*) market in Turkey which is overseen and regulated by the Directorate General of Insurance, (T.C. Basbakanlik Hazine Müstesarligi, Inönü Bulvari No 36, 06510 Emek, Ankara; Tel +90 312 204 6000; Fax +90 312 212 8871; www.sigortacilik. gov.tr). There are over 50 active insurance companies in the country, including a number of international companies, which offer a variety of services. Not all the companies offer insurance in all categories, with fewer than 30 offering health insurance.

Most expatriates are likely to require vehicle insurance and health (*sağlık*) insurance, which may well be best bought from a Turkish provider. If you buy property you will also need to purchase mandatory earthquake (DASK) insurance. All property insurance must be purchased from a company registered and authorised to operate in Turkey.

All the insurance companies active in Turkey are members of the Association of the Insurance and Reinsurance Companies of Turkey (Büyükdere St., Büyükdere Plaza No 195, Floor:1-2 34394, Levent, Istanbul; Tel +90 212 324 1950; Fax +90 212 325 6108; genel@tsrsb. org.tr; www.tsrsb.org.tr).

In addition to the insurance companies there are insurance agents who represent specific companies, insurance brokers who represent a number of companies and insurance experts who assess damage on behalf of the insurance companies in the event of a claim. The insurance agents and brokers are regulated by law and insurance specialists undertake specific training and are required to pass professional exams.

TAXES (TURKEY)

Taxes are levied in Turkey both directly and indirectly. Direct taxes are income-based and apply to individuals and companies. Indirect taxes include VAT, stamp duty and motoring taxes.

Personal Income Tax

Personal income tax is levied on all sources of income, including business profits, salary income, agricultural income, provision of services when self-employed, rental income from property and income from investments.

If you are resident in Turkey your worldwide income will be deemed as taxable in Turkey. Residency is determined as your normal place of residence, or residency of more than six months in Turkey within any year.

Non-residents may also be liable to Turkish tax on any income generated in Turkey from sources such as property, investments or business. In certain circumstances Turkish nationals may be liable for Turkish taxes whilst living and working outside the country.

When determining the level of salary and wages that is taxable, all bonuses, commissions, gratuities and similar payments are included in the gross amount. The net taxable value, however, allows for deductions relating to such expenses as insurances, pensions and union membership.

Where income derives from self-employment, allowable expenses can be deducted from gross income to determine the net taxable income. Allowable deductions include:

- rental of premises;
- overheads;
- utilities relating to the work;
- salaries of agency staff and associated fees;
- cost of manuals, journals and related professional publications;
- membership of professional associations;
- work-related travel and subsistence expenses;

- cost of tools, equipment, and materials required;
- depreciation of assets;
- pension contributions;
- contractual losses.

Where income is derived from so-called immovable property, such property includes not only buildings and land, but identifiable assets such as intellectual property and commercial vehicles. The net taxable income from revenue derived in this way allows for deductions, restoration, maintenance, management, depreciation and running costs. Alternatively, instead of calculating an accounting value for the costs associated with rental income, a lump sum of 25% of gross income can be used as a deduction.

Movable property is broadly defined as stocks, shares, bonds and other financial investments that offer a cash dividend or the opportunity for capital appreciation. Deductions from the gross income can be made for collection costs, insurance costs and non-income related taxes.

Capital gains are taxed as specific income and the costs of realising the capital gain can be deducted from the gross amount to determine the taxable income. Gains from the increase in the value of property are subject to capital gains tax if sold within five years for properties bought after January 1st 2007, or four years if bought before that date.

Taxes on business income are only due if the business has a permanent presence in Turkey through an office or representative and revenue is generated directly by this presence. Income is determined to be from a business if you carry on that business regularly, as opposed to intermittently. If you only work occasionally the income will be deemed as miscellaneous income and not subject to the rules relating to business income and expenses.

Certain expenses can be deducted from the gross income to determine the net income liable for tax and, whilst not an exhaustive list, the following are examples of what can be deducted:

- board and lodgings for employees on company premises or sites;

- medical expenses incurred as a result of work activities;
- insurance and pension payments;
- cost of clothing provided for employees;
- certain costs, damages payments and indemnities due as a result of business activities;
- travel, accommodation and other expenses;
- commercial vehicle expenses;
- taxes, fees and charges levied by government and other organisation as a result of carrying on the business;
- depreciation of capital equipment.

Expenses that cannot be included to reduce tax liabilities:

- money, other assets, or payment in kind received by the owner, spouse or children;
- salaries, wages, bonuses, commissions or other financial compensation paid to the owner, a spouse, or the owner's children;
- interest payments on any capital investment made by the owner;
- fines and tax penalties as a result of unlawful actions;
- advertising of alcoholic drinks or tobacco.

Agricultural income is any income gained from farming, hunting, fishing, horticulture or similar activities, whether the activity is onshore or on the water. Additionally, using agricultural equipment on a third party's farm, for payment, is deemed as agricultural income.

Small farmers with an income of less than a certain government-specified amount, which is set annually, are exempt from tax on agricultural income altogether. Farmers whose income is above this amount fall into two further categories. Either their expenses are considered to be 80% of income for animal products and 70% of income for other produce, or if they earn above a second government-specified amount, their expenses need to be accounted for. Allowable expenses are similar to those allowed for other businesses as listed above.

For 2008 the personal tax rates are as below, with a tax free allowance of YTL2,400 allowable for allocation against rental income from residential buildings:

Taxable Amount	Income Tax Due
YTL0 to YTL7,800	15% of taxable amount
YTL7801 to YTL19,800	YTL1,170 from above, plus 20% of the rest
YTL19,800 to YTL44,700	YTL3570 from above, plus 27% of the rest
YTL44,700 upwards	YTL10,293 from above, plus 35% of the rest

Corporation Taxes

Corporation tax covers the income derived by traditional companies, cooperatives, publicly-owned companies, joint ventures and businesses owned and run by associations and similar organisations.

Businesses that are deemed to have unlimited liability for Turkish taxes on their worldwide income are those whose registered head office is in Turkey, or one that is deemed to carry out its principle management activities in Turkey. Otherwise, only that income derived in Turkey is liable for Turkish taxes.

Tax is liable on the net increase in the value of the company, most often measured as the net revenue earned by the company, unless the fixed assets have increased in value.

Income paid to partners in a partnership is deemed to be personal business income and reference should be made to the relevant section above for further information on partnership tax issues. However, profit within the partnership can still be taxed.

Allowable expenses that can be deducted from the gross income are similar to those listed under personal business income above. In addition, a company can also deduct, where applicable, the following expenses:

- set up costs of the business;
- cost of issuing shares in the business;

- costs associated with a merger, dissolution, and liquidation;
- board meeting expenses;
- share options or profit share bonuses to partners in a partnership;
- certain costs associated with research and development and bringing new technology to the market.

Companies are required to file annual tax returns in accordance with the rules in force at the time and within a specified period which depends on the status of the company and type of revenue earned.

The corporate tax rate is 20% and withholding tax is held on revenue earned by non-residents earning income from the sale of licences, intellectual property or other assets, or companies with no presence in Turkey.

Indirect Taxation

There are a number of indirect taxes in Turkey, which generally correspond to those in place elsewhere in Europe. Value Added Tax, or VAT (*katma değer vergisi*, KDV), is the main indirect tax that affects everyone. Other taxes include stamp duty, vehicle tax, banking and insurance taxes, gambling tax, inheritance/gift tax, property tax, communications tax, education contribution fee, import duty and a special consumption tax.

VAT is levied on the sale, lease and importation of all goods and services, whether by an individual, partnership or company. In some cases the transportation of a commodity across Turkey will result in tax being due.

VAT is collected at the point of every transaction until the final sale. However, the amount of tax due to be paid to the government by the collecting person or entity is the difference between the amount of VAT paid out on purchases and the amount of VAT collected on any sale.

Where the person or company making the sale is not present, or does not have a place of business in Turkey, the person making the transaction on behalf of the individual or company is liable for ensuring the correct tax is paid to the government.

VAT is payable on the full value of the product or service involved and where no payment is made, the VAT is still due and is calculated on the open market value as determined by the Ministry of Finance.

The standard rate of VAT in Turkey is 18%, though there are discounted rates for some foodstuffs, agricultural produce, books and leased items. The discounted rates are 1% and 8%.

Stamp duty is paid on contracts, financial instruments and other documentation and the rate varies from 0.15% (rent) to 0.75% (value of a contract) and the liability is defined by law for each occurrence.

Motor vehicle tax is levied annually on all types of vehicle and the rates are outlined in more detail in Chapter 3.

Banking and insurance tax is paid directly by banks, insurance companies and other finance companies on the revenue they earn from the transactions they carry out, and the institutions are liable for the tax on a monthly basis. The tax rate is fixed at 5%.

Gambling tax is paid by the operators of all betting activity, including lotteries, bingo and other gambling-type activities. The rates depend on the activity concerned and is paid monthly.

Inheritance and gift tax are progressive taxes with gift tax ranging from 10% to 30% and inheritance tax ranging from 1% to 10% of the item's value. Where the item was gifted or inherited outside of Turkey the tax paid outside of Turkey will be deducted from the amount due in Turkey itself. Any tax due can be paid in instalments over a three year period.

Where a spouse and children inherit property, the first YTL96,000 in value of the property is tax free, whilst where a spouse only inherits a property then YTL192,000 is tax free. For gifts, the tax-free allowance is YTL2,200.

Taxable Amount	Inheritance Tax	Gift Tax
Up to YTL150,000	1%	10%
YTL150,001 to YTL470,000	3%	15%

YTL470.001 to YTL1,150,000	5%	20%
YTL1,150,001 to YTL2,530,000	7%	25%
YTL2,530,001 and above	10%	30%

Property taxes are paid annually in two instalments on the value of a property, based on the declared value at the last point of sale, the value declared in a property tax return, or as amended by government at any time and range from 0.1% to 0.3% depending on the whether the property is land, domestic, commercial or development property.

Property sales tax is charged at 1.5% of the declared value of a property at the point of sale and paid by both the buyer and the seller.

An environmental services tax is levied on water supplied to domestic and commercial buildings. In rural areas the domestic tax is YTL0.13 per cubic metre and YTL0.16 in urban areas. Commercial rates are fixed sums ranging from YTL10 to YTL2,000 depending on the premises.

Communication tax is charged on the fixed equipment, operation and communications activity of mobile phone operators at 25% on the same basis as VAT is charged on other products or services.

A temporary education contribution fee is being collected until 2010 to fund the improvements required in the education system to ensure all primary children can receive free education and particularly to improve the rate of girls attending full-time primary education. The fee is collected from certain commercial transactions as a fixed levy.

Customs duty is collected on goods imported from abroad that are subject to the tax. The person declaring the goods for import (e.g. the import agent) is liable for the tax, which is based on a written declaration and must be paid within ten days of the declaration.

A special consumption tax is due on a number of specific products only once during the sale cycle of the products. A non-exclusive list of products involved is shown below.

• Petroleum and petroleum-related products and derivatives where the tax is payable by the manufacturer and importer of the products.

- Motor vehicles, motorcycles, planes, helicopters and boats where the tax is payable by the retailer, exporter, or seller at auction.

- Tobacco and tobacco products where the tax is payable by the manufacturer, exporter, or seller at auction.

- Alcoholic drinks and cola where the tax is payable by the manufacturer, exporter, or seller at auction.

- Specified luxury products where the tax is payable by the manufacturer, exporter, or seller at auction.

Further information on taxation can be obtained from the General Directorate of Revenues (Gelir Idaresi Başkanliği), Ilkadim Cad. 06450, Dikmen, Ankara; Tel +90 312 415 2900; Fax +90 312 415 2821; www.gib.gov.tr.

TAXES (HOME COUNTRY)

Australia

If Australians are resident abroad for an unbroken period of 91 days then their foreign income from employment is exempt from Australian taxation, as long as tax is paid in the foreign country. Home leave is generally not considered as a break in the required period as long as such holidays are not excessive.

Self-employment or delivery of independent services is not considered as employment and therefore the exemption may not apply. Where a country does not levy income tax itself (e.g. Saudi Arabia) you will be liable for Australian tax.

A declaration that you are living outside of Australia will be required to claim a tax exemption and further information can be obtained from the Australian Tax Office, GPO Box 9990 in the capital city of your home state/territory; www.ato.gov.au; Tel 13 28 61; International Tel +61 2 6216 1111.

Canada

If you are deemed to have Canadian residency then you are likely to be liable for Canadian tax on your Turkish income. As Canada does not have a tax treaty with Turkey you will be classed as a factual resident of Canada and be required to file a Canadian tax return detailing your worldwide income. You will, however, be able to claim foreign tax credit on any tax paid in Turkey, which will reduce your Canadian liability.

Further information on the Canadian tax system can be obtained from any Canadian Embassy, or the International Tax Services Office, Canada Revenue Agency, 2204 Walkley Road, Ottawa ON K1A 1A8, Canada; www.cra-arc.gc.ca; calls from Canada and the US 1 800 267 5177; calls from outside Canada and the US +1 613 952 3741.

New Zealand

If you live and/or work outside of New Zealand for more than 325 days in a 12-month period, you may become non-resident for tax purposes, unless you have an enduring link to New Zealand. Any social, economic, property or accommodation ties would place you in this category.

If you are deemed to have a continuing tie with the country then you will remain resident for tax purposes. You will therefore be liable to pay New Zealand tax on all your worldwide income unless the country you are living in has a tax treaty with New Zealand. Turkey has no tax treaty with New Zealand.

Further information can be obtained by writing to your nearest Inland Revenue office (www.ird.govt.nz):

- Inland Revenue, P.O.Box 1477, Waikato Mail Centre, Hamilton 3240;
- Inland Revenue, P.O.Box 39010, Wellington Mail Centre, Lower Hutt 5045;
- Inland Revenue, P.O.Box 3753, Christchurch Mail Centre, Christchurch 8140;

or by calling the advice lines:

- Telephone call from within New Zealand; 0800 227 774;
- Telephone call from outside New Zealand; +64 4 978 0779.

USA

The USA and Turkey have a tax treaty primarily to ensure the avoidance of double taxation. However, US citizens and resident aliens living abroad must still file a US tax return, estate tax return and gift tax return and pay estimated taxes as if resident in the USA.

You will be taxable on your worldwide income, unless you claim a tax credit or an itemised deduction based on the tax you have already paid on the overseas-generated income. If you choose to make a deduction of your foreign source income you cannot then make a claim for credit on any tax paid overseas.

A foreign tax credit can only be claimed under certain circumstances including:

- the tax must be imposed by the foreign government;
- the tax must actually be paid or accounted for;
- the tax must be a legal and actual foreign tax liability;
- the tax must be income based.

In general terms only income- and revenue-based taxes can be claimed for foreign tax credits, though these usually include wages, company dividends, savings interest, and royalty payments. All international tax returns must be filed at the Internal Revenue Service Center, Austin, TX 73301-0215, USA, if you are claiming any foreign tax credits or tax residency in another country.

If you are claiming no foreign or international entitlements then you should file your tax return in the normal way at the address listed on the filing form.

Filings following the calendar year must be submitted by April 15th of the year following the end of the tax year of the return. Fiscal-year based returns are due three months and 15 days following the end of the fiscal year. Any tax due should be paid by the date the tax return is due.

Taxpayers based outside the USA can contact the Internal Revenue Service by mail at P.O. Box 920, Bensalem, PA 19020, USA; Tel +1 215 516 2000 (not toll-free); Fax: +1 215 516 2555; www.irs.gov.

UK

British citizens leaving the UK to live and/or work abroad should complete form P85 and return it to their tax office to ensure their tax status is accurately determined. As UK tax is calculated on your earnings whilst resident in the country you may be eligible for a tax refund if you have been paying tax on a salary or other income and you then leave part way through the tax year.

Income arising in the UK whilst you are resident abroad is taxable in the UK unless you are transferring the income to another taxation authority under a tax treaty. However, for couples where only one partner is working, this UK tax liability can be very useful as the UK tax allowances can be claimed on any UK income. If the non-working partner declares income such as house rental is coming to them, they can use their tax allowance to offset and reduce any liability. To claim this allowance form R43 must be completed and returned to Her Majesty Revenue and Customs, HMRC Residency, Fitz Roy House, P.O.Box 46, Nottingham, United Kingdom NG2 1BD.

If you are non-resident in the UK and have no income arising in the UK then it is not usually necessary to complete and submit a Self Assessment Tax Return, though if you are already required to submit these then it is possible you will need to do so after leaving the UK. Completion of form P85 as discussed above will help ensure you keep up to date with your UK tax liabilities.

Where you have savings with a bank or building society in the UK you can receive interest on that money tax free by completing HMRC form R105 and sending it to your bank or building society. Additionally, the UK and Turkey have a tax treaty that covers income and other personal taxes to help ensure there is no dual taxation to worry about.

All HMRC forms are available online at www.hmrc.gov.uk and further information is available from any UK HMRC office, from the website, or by phone from within the UK on 0845 070 0040, or from outside the UK on +44 151 210 2222.

Ireland

As an Irish national or other nationality with Irish domicility but not resident in Ireland, you will be liable for Irish taxes on all your worldwide income, except earned income coming from a salary or self-employment arising from activity carried out wholly outside of Ireland.

Turkey and Ireland do not have a tax treaty limiting liability for taxes to one country, but one is under negotiation at the time of writing. Income arising in Turkey will therefore be liable for Irish taxation net of any tax paid in Turkey. Once the treaty is in place it should allow for any Turkish tax to be discounted from Irish tax liability.

Further information can be obtained from your local Revenue tax office or the office of Collector General (Sarsfield House, Francis Street, Limerick; Tel 1890 20 30 70; Tel +353 61 488 000 (for international callers); www.revenue.ie; cg@revenue.ie) also handles international claims.

OFFSHORE BANKING

Offshore banking is a term often applied to the services offered by banks in the so-called tax havens of the world to individuals and companies that are based elsewhere in the world. In the UK the term 'offshore' arose as a description of such services as the favourite locations for Britons were Jersey, Guernsey, the Isle of Man and Gibraltar, which were all offshore from the UK. Other landlocked providers in Europe are based in Switzerland, Luxembourg and Lichtenstein, whilst elsewhere the Virgin Islands and the Seychelles are favoured locations.

In reality, offshore banking is any financial service provided to an individual or a company from an institution in a country other than where the customer is resident or based. The institution does not necessarily have to be based in a tax-haven as there may be many reasons for the use of such services over and above the limiting of tax liabilities.

For expatriates the use of specialist offshore banking services can be for facilitating access to funds anywhere in the world, security of deposits if they are living in a financially-unstable country, or stable banking services whilst they move frequently from country to country.

The process of opening of an offshore bank account is similar to that of opening a traditional account. You will usually need to provide proof of identity, proof of address, bank references, proof of income and if you are depositing a large sum of money you will generally be required to demonstrate that it comes from a reputable source. Where you are opening an account at a distance then you will need to provide a certified copy of your proof of identity.

Many European and international banks have offshore operations specifically for expatriates and these can be accessed through their onshore branches, who will usually facilitate the opening of an offshore account. If you already have a UK or other European account you may well find that the bank can set up an offshore account for you via your local branch.

Larger international banks also have offshore operations around the world and can provide a sense of comfort that your money is in safe hands as you travel the world.

Banks offering services to expatriates from recognised offshore countries and territories will offer the full range of retail banking services. Where requested, the accounts will come with a debit card, cheque book, internet and telephone banking, statements, direct debits and standing orders.

Additional services offered by the banks can include overdraft facilities, loans, credit cards, mortgages, wealth management and pension planning. Some of the banks will also offer insurance services and other financial services.

10
Travel and Leisure

There is plenty to see and do in Turkey, whether you want sport, entertainment, culture or relaxation. With such a wealth of history, culture, cities, countryside, mountains and coastline to choose from there should be something to keep people of all tastes and interests occupied.

To fully enjoy all that is on offer it helps to have friends and acquaintances in both the expat and the Turkish community who can advise what is on offer, make introductions or give directions to the hidden places that usually offer the best experiences.

This chapter covers some of the most well-known and easily accessible transport and leisure options to get you started on your Turkish experience. As you get to know your way around and gain confidence in your ability to communicate with people and enjoy Turkey, you will find places not listed below or in the guide books. It is these experiences and places that can make your time in Turkey one that is truly enjoyable and memorable.

GETTING AROUND

For such a large country, with some very large cities and the huge metropolis that is Istanbul, Turkey is relatively easy to get around. It may not always be fast, but the public transport services can be comprehensive, well-connected, cheap and get you pretty much everywhere you want to go.

The roads sometimes leave a lot to be desired, but that can make them even more spectacular. From high mountain passes, across long Anatolian plains, to scenic coastal routes, the travelling is as variable as the country.

Whether you are driving yourself, travelling by bus, enjoying a lazy train trip or catching a flight, the whole experience of moving around the country usually adds something to the trip.

Local Buses (*otobüsü*)

Local bus services are operated by the local government authority and termed municipality bus (*belediye otobüsü*) or by a privately run operator and known as the *halk otobüsü*. Though providing a cheap, but regular and far reaching service, they can be slow, uncomfortable, noisy and crowded. If you are not familiar with a city or a route it can also be difficult to know which bus to take and where to get on or off.

The *belediye otobüsü* often require pre-paid tickets to be bought before getting on the bus, while the *halk otobüsü* are more likely to require cash when you board the vehicle. Unless reducing costs is a prime concern, few foreigners use local buses.

Taxi (*taksi*)

Bright yellow taxis are a common sight in Turkey. They are cheap, convenient and accessible as they will generally stop if they are empty and you try and flag them down.

Taxi ranks can be found at large hotels, airports, bus and train stations and at strategic (though not always obvious) locations in towns and cities. You can also telephone for a taxi to pick you up and take you to another location and some taxis operate an informal delivery service for shops and restaurants.

All taxis are metered and there are specific rules on charging for extras such as luggage, road tolls, waiting periods and night fares. Always check to make sure the meter is turned on at the start of a journey and ensure the driver is absolutely clear as to where you want to go (especially if you are not confident of your Turkish language skills).

Dolmuş

Dolmuş are a quintessentially Turkish mode of transport, with their name being a result of how they operate. *Dolmuş* means 'stuffed' in Turkish, and they usually are. *Dolmuş* are small mini-bus type vehicles that are very box-like in style and reminiscent of 1960s passsenger vehicles. Newer versions are less dated-looking, but close in style to the hundreds of traditional vehicles still plying their trade. In each area all the *dolmuş* will be painted in the same colours.

They operate fixed routes, with the destination on a board in the front window, and they generally wait until they are full before setting off, then collect more passengers along the way. When full, the fares are passed from passenger to passenger until it reaches the driver, with change rarely coming back, so try and see what everyone else is paying and pass along the correct change.

For short journeys, or for experiencing local life and colour, they are a great way to travel. They are also good when you are in a hurry as they stop for as short a time as possible to allow passengers on and off and travel as fast as the driver can make them go.

Underground (*Metro*)

There are underground *metro* systems in Ankara, Izmir and Istanbul, with two linked systems operating in Istanbul and Ankara.

In Ankara the system is limited and the two systems are the *metro* and the newer Ankaray. The *metro* runs from Kizilay to Batıkent, while the Ankaray starts at the AŞTİ bus terminal and terminates at Dikmenevi. The two services link at Kizilay in the centre of Ankara and Ankaray also links to the local suburban train service (*banliyö treni*) at Maltepe and Kurtuluş. Multi-journey tickets as well as single trip tickets can be bought for both services.

In Istanbul the *metro* system is run by the Istanbul Transportation Company (Istanbul Ulaşım Transportation Co.) and offers a more extensive system than that on offer in the capital Ankara. Istanbul's *metro* system is still under construction and the archaeological challenge of digging under Istanbul has been met with a determination to improve services in the city whilst protecting the wealth of finds recovered in the process. Some stations even have exhibits of the archaeological artefacts recovered whilst digging out the platform. The most convenient way to travel on the *metro* is to use the Akbil system described below. The main line runs from Atatürk Airport to Aksaray where it connects with the tramway system and other modes of transport.

Izmir's *metro* system is undergoing improvement work to its seven mile length to extend it up to an effective length of 50 miles in the future, which will see it run around the Gulf of Izmir and connect the northern and southern suburbs to each other, the city and the airport and interlink with the suburban rail network.

Trams

There are two tramways in Istanbul, one is very short and the other is much longer and runs from east to west across the European side of the city. There is also a funicular train system connecting the tramway to the Bosphorus.

The shorter route runs between Taksım and Tünel along the pedestrianised Istiklal Çaddesi. Tickets are usually bought before boarding, or you can use your Akbil (see page 152). The system is over 130 years old and one of the icons of old Istanbul.

There are nine miles of tramway between Kabataş and Zeytinburnu that were the original length of this line, which was then extended to Bağcılar. The complete line is a modern and quick mode of transport that links in with the Hafif *metro* system at the Zeytinburnu and Aksaray stations. An information website on the history of the Istanbul trams and the modern route is at: www.dersaadettramvayi.com.

Between Taksım and Kabataş is a funicular (*füniküler*) railway system that links the tramway above with the Kabataş ferry port and the Taksım to Levent *metro*. Single journey tickets can be bought for this or you can use your Akbil card.

Local and Light Train Services

Most towns and cities have local train services to complement the inter-city routes, but in Izmir, Istanbul and Ankara there are specific suburban train services (*banliyö treni*) for commuters and residents of the large urban areas.

In Istanbul the route on the northern shore of the Bosphorus runs from Sirkeci station (where trains from Europe arrive) out past the airport to Halkali on the shores of the Sea of Marmara. The closest station to the airport is Yeşilyurt, approximately ten minutes by taxi.

On the Asian side of the Bosphorus the train runs from Haydarpaşa Station out to Gebze on the south side of the sea of Marmara, passing through Fenerbaçhe for those interested in football.

In Ankara the local train runs from Sincan in the west to the main station (Ankara Gar) and out to Kayaş in the east. The trains are often full, noisy and slow, but cheap and reliable which is why they are so popular.

The local Izmir trains will, once work is completed, integrate with the tram system and become a comprehensive and effective way of travelling around the large conurbation that is Turkey's third largest city.

Akbil

Akbil, which means 'smart ticket', is a ticketing system valid on all buses, ferries and *metro* systems in Istanbul and gives you a discount of up to 25% on fares. Akbils come in a variety of different colours and the key-sized fobs can be bought from Akbil kiosks (Akbil Satiş Noktasi) at major bus stops for less than 10YTL; you can then buy credit depending on your needs. There are Akbil top up points at major bus stops, ferry ports and other public transport locations.

Long-distance Buses

Travelling by bus in Turkey is easy, relatively cheap, comfortable and, with a network that stretches to just about every city, town and village, also highly convenient.

The number of bus companies is bewildering. Some operators serve only local destinations, others only one long-distance route. There are also a few major operators who have extensive route networks and run large fleets of buses on complex, inter-linked timetables.

Bus travel is the most popular mode of transport for Turks and the infrastructure to serve this huge operation is comprehensive and impressive. Some of the main bus terminals were, until recently, more like airport terminals than the airport terminals of Istanbul and Ankara, and are a pleasure to use when compared to the dirty and dark bus stations elsewhere in Europe and Asia.

The main bus terminal in Istanbul is on the European side of the Bosphorus and officially called the Esenler Otobüs Terminal, but it is more commonly known as the *büyük otogar* (big bus station) and has scores of ticket windows and departure bays. On the Asian side of the Bosphorus is the Harem Terminal in Üsküdar. The main terminal in Ankara is known as the AŞTİ Terminal and is a circular glass and steel building worthy of any international airport.

Every town and city will have a centrally-located bus terminal as will every village. Away from the big cities and popular tourist places, these terminals are not so grand, but they are functional and busy. In smaller towns and villages, though, the village square may serve as the terminal with tickets sold from a kiosk or bought on board the bus.

Some of the larger operators have, however, gone out on their own and run their services between dedicated terminal buildings away from the main bus stations. These can be quieter and also be served with local courtesy buses to get you to your final destination, so they can be worth considering even though they may be more expensive.

Once on the bus there will be stops every two hours for refreshments and comfort breaks. Smoking is not allowed on the buses and there are rarely toilets on board, so it is well worth taking advantage of the facilities available at each stop. Rest stops are usually taken at well equipped service stations where a shop, restaurant, toilets and other facilities are available.

Though there are scores of bus operators some are more reliable and have a better name for safety on the notoriously dangerous Turkish roads. Whilst they may be more expensive, comfort, safety, reliability and more frequent services can be worth paying for.

Tickets can be bought in advance, or at the terminal immediately before departure. Some of the larger operators also sell tickets online (occasionally with an online discount), though others have no website at all.

An alternative to the traditional point-to-point ticket is a hop-on hop-off service. The Fez Bus, operated by Fez Travel (www.feztravel.com) runs from June to October and one ticket allows you to break your journey at any point on the route to see what you want for as long as you want. The bus runs every two days from each departure point and offers a great circular route around some of the most popular destinations in the country as well as some branch routes to additional destinations.

Long Distance Train

The intercity train services in Turkey are run by Turkish State Railways (Türkiye Cumhuriyeti Devlet Demiryollari, TCDD) on behalf of the Ministry of Transport. The first route was started in 1856 when a British company began building the line from Izmir to Aydin. The network now stretches across the country along just under 11,000 kilometres of track, with most of the routes single line operation.

Historically the trains have been a scenic, but slow, method of travel between the cities of Turkey. However, a programme of upgrading and transformation of the old, slow intercity routes began in 2003 with the Ankara to Istanbul line. The intention is to halve the journey time to a little over three hours from the current six to seven hours. In 2006 work began on a high speed Konya to Ankara route connecting with the Ankara line at a point roughly half way to Eskişehir at Polatlı. Further improvements to the network are planned throughout the country and a joint venture train factory, with South Korean technology, has been established to build the new high speed trains that will use the improved infrastructure.

As the improvements come to fruition the train network will become a viable alternative to flying for those pressed for time, but some of the relaxing pleasures of taking the night train to Istanbul from Ankara and arriving for sunrise on the Bosphorus will have gone.

The network is extensive and there are sleeping cars, couchettes, restaurant cars and traditional seating arrangements depending on the route and your budget. First and second class options are also available, as are discounts for students and the elderly.

Tickets must be bought in advance and for some popular routes and especially during holiday periods this must be done weeks before travelling. Route, pricing and ticketing information is available on the website (www.tcdd.gov.tr) under the Passenger Transportation menu button, though it can be difficult to find.

For train buffs there are also several train museums and exhibitions in Izmir, Ankara and Istanbul, further information on these can also be found on the TCDD website.

Ferry

A variety of domestic ferry routes ply back and forth across the Bosphorius, the Dardanelles and the Gulf of Izmir. They have featured in numerous advertising campaigns to promote Turkey as a tourist destination, but primarily they are for commuters going back and forth to work.

In Istanbul there are many boats of different types working the waterways. Boats in a variety of sizes cross back and forth across the Bosphorus, or run longer trips along the shoreline. Routes run from Kadıköy, Eminönü, Beşiktaş, Haydarpaşa, Üsküdar, Karaköy and other points. With services being offered by both the municipality-operated Istanbul Deniz Otobüsleri and a private group under the banner of TURYOL. The larger catamarans operate the sea bus (*deniz otobüsü*) routes that are usually longer, or operate during rush hour. Spreading out through the Sea of Marmara these fast boats go as far as Yalova and Bandırma to serve Bursa and Çannakale.

A longer-distance service runs between Istanbul and Bodrum, stopping at Çesme, a popular spa resort for Turkish holidaymakers and second-homeowners. Operated by DenizLine (www.denizline.com.tr), these mini-cruises run during the summer and offer a more relaxed way to travel the Aegean coastal route.

A number of ferries cross the Dardanelles with the main car ferry routes from Çanakkale to Eceabat and Gelibolu to Lapseki and the smaller car ferry between Çanakkale and Kilitbahir. Other services operate from Bozcaada to Odunluk, Çanakkale to Gökçeada and Kabatepe to Gökçeada. There are numerous sailings, with more in the summer and they provide an excellent route for people driving from Europe to the Mediterranean as well as Southern Anatolia.

In Izmir there are municipal ferries plying back and forth across the Gulf of Izmir that interconnect with the train and bus services in an integrated public transport system, coordinated by a single body. There are eight landing points: Alsancak, Bayraklı, Bostanlı, Göztepe, Karşıyaka, Konak, Pasaport and Üçkuyular. Under development at the time of writing is the website of the ferry operator Izmir Denizcilic Işletmeleri.

Plane

Internal flights in Turkey can often make sense in terms of speed and budget as advance booking can see prices remarkably low considering the huge distances travelled and the time saved when compared to bus or train travel.

Turkish Airlines (Türk Hava Yollar, THY) operate numerous domestic services to complement their international routes and they compare well with any international airline for in-flight service and comfort. They can also be cheap, but would fall into the category of mid- to low-price rather than budget.

There are other airlines operating domestic services in Turkey with bases away from Istanbul. The German airline Sun Express operates mostly from Izmir, but with a wide range of domestic routes to feed into international flights to Germany and Austria. Izair are based in Izmir but also operate flights between other domestic airports. AtlasJet are based in Istanbul and operate both domestic routes as well as international services to a number of countries. OnurAir was one of the earliest competitors to Turkish Airlines and also operates domestic and international flights from an Istanbul base.

Car

Travelling by car gives you freedom to explore and stop where you want to. It can isolate you from other travellers, though sometimes the peace and quiet can be welcome. The road network is extensive and the quality of the roads is improving all the time with new motorways and other improvements across the country.

Acclimatisation to the Turkish driving style can be a challenge for some. Patience is in short supply with Turkish drivers and they will try to squeeze into the smallest space on the road if they think it will get them to their destination any quicker.

The accident rate is high and driving at night is not recommended as that is when many of the lorries travel, which are well known for overtaking on blind corners and not using their headlights. They are also notorious for parking in unlit streets without any lights on.

Some people say you should drive defensively, but perhaps it may be better to drive assertively. Either way, confidence and a strong nerve are required in the cities as well as concentration when driving along endless miles of straight road in central Anatolia.

Unless you take your own car, renting will be necessary. Both chauffeured and self-drive cars are available and local rental firms compete effectively with the large international operators. Pricing and the model of car can vary significantly, with some local operators offering cars of dubious quality and safety and little in the way of insurance cover. Using a reputable car hire company is well worth the higher fees.

The road signs and rules of the road are based on international standards and are covered in Chapter 3. Fuel stations and repair centres are widely available and independent garages can sort out just about any problem and get you on your way even in the most remote parts of the country.

On the whole, driving in the remoter parts of Turkey can be a joy and take you to places you might never get the chance to see if you stick to public transport.

LEISURE ACTIVITIES

Golf

Golf has become a major industry in Turkey, not only in terms of the sport itself, but also the spin-offs. Around Belek, near Antalya, there are numerous golf courses of international standard and to complement these are hotels, apartment and villa developments and resort complexes to cater for the golfers, their families and friends. They offer far more than just golf.

Golf is strongly supported by the government as a means of promoting the country and attracting both tourism and investment to the country. The Turkish Golf Federation was set up to support the development of golf in the country and to ensure high standards prevail in the industry.

Along the Mediterranean coast there are 14 golf clubs in place or under development, stretching as far as Lykia in the east. The weather and the views make golfing in this region of Turkey particularly pleasurable. Whether you are looking for a coastal links course, green wooded courses, or stunning views of the mountains, the options are there for you.

Elsewhere in Turkey there are two courses in Istanbul at the Kemer Golf and Country Club and the Klassis Golf and Country Club.

New courses are also under development at Kızılçahamam near Ankara, Muğla, Bodrum (designed by Gary Player) and Aydın. A third Istanbul course is planned for Pendık. The charges for a round can be as low as £19 (US$40) for guests staying at accommodation linked to the courses, going up to £70 (US$140) for visitors.

Full details of the Antalya and Mediterranean golf courses, both those in operation and under development, can be found on the website of the tour operator Turkish Golf (www.turkishgolf.com).

In Ankara there is also the Golf International Friendship Society Golf Sports Club for Turkish and foreign diplomats to promote golf in Turkey, which has a driving range and offers golf lessons.

A website promoting golf in Turkey to an international audience and providing news and updates on the Turkish golf scene can be found at www.golf.com.tr.

Walking

Walking, or trekking, has traditionally not been a popular pastime for Turks. Neither has it been a popular tourist activity, which is surprising given the beautiful scenery, large areas of relatively empty space and the mountain ranges spread across the country.

In recent years there has been an effort to increase the number of outdoor activities available that do not depend on the sea. Golf saw the first major burst of activity, then skiing, now walking has begun to receive attention.

Cappadocia is a popular destination with independent travellers and the restrictions on vehicular access to many of the valleys attractive to tourists have resulted in a number of relatively short and easy walking routes being set up to allow access to the better sites.

The ten mile long Ihlara Valley, located seven miles from Aksaray, is a highlight of walking in Cappadocia. It is a 100m deep canyon, fed by the Melendiz River, that hosts houses, churches and rock-carved tombs, interconnected by tunnels running through the valley walls.

Elsewhere in Cappadocia it is possible to walk through the hills and along the valleys between the towns, but the routes are not marked and joining a guided tour can make the hikes easier and more enjoyable with the added input of a knowledgeable guide.

The Lycian Way is a 300 mile route along the coast from Fethiye to

Antalya. Increasing in difficulty the further you get from Fethiye, the route is classed as moderate to difficult, and the extreme heat in the summer limits the time when it is practical to walk it. The Lycian Way was researched and planned by Kate Clow with Terry Richardson and implemented with the support of volunteers and sponsored by Garanti Bank.

St Paul's Trail is a new long-distance route opened in 2004, running from Perge to Yalvac, with a branch out to Aspendos along the way. The total route is approximately 300 miles and was also researched and planned by Kate Clow with Terry Richardson and implemented with the support of volunteers and sponsored by Exodus travel and other trekking companies.

For the more adventurous there is serious hiking in the Taurus mountains, the Kaçkar mountains, on Mount Ağri (Ararat) and in the national parks. Facilities are usually limited and you will need to take a tent and carry your own food for when you are unable to find accommodation along the way.

Gardening

Gardening in Turkey must be suited to the weather. With such extremes of heat, cold, dry and wetness, depending on where you are, choosing your plants carefully will be essential to producing a good display. With the internet, finding information on gardening and suitable plants for the Turkish climate will not be a problem, but sourcing plants may be more difficult.

The importation of plants will require a phyto-sanitary certificate, but seed can be brought in easily. Gardening is not a popular hobby in Turkey, with gardens historically reserved for the rich and aristocratic who enjoyed the gardens rather than worked them.

As the original home of the tulip and with the hills covered in wild roses, there are plenty of wild and native plants to learn about and, if desired, cultivate.

One advantage of the hot climate is the chance to grow Mediterranean produce. Peppers, tomatoes, melons and other local delicacies thrive with the summer heat and some added water and can be grown to provide a most enjoyable supplement to your diet.

Cinema

The cinema is a popular activity in Turkey and there is one in every town and city. In the larger cities there are modern multiplex cinemas that show international films, often with subtitles rather than being dubbed into Turkish.

For the connoisseur there are a number of international film festivals, the most important being the Antalya Golden Orange Film Festival, the Istanbul Film Festival and the Ankara International Film Festival.

Sports

Sports facilities have become increasingly available in Turkey, primarily as a result of the demand from a growing and increasingly wealthy group of middle class Turks. The number of private sports clubs has boomed and they offer excellent facilities at reasonable prices.

The bigger clubs offer swimming, squash, tennis, badminton, and other sports along with fitness suites, saunas and cafés. A leading example is Sports International with five clubs in Ankara, Istanbul and Izmir.

Skiing

There are a dozen resorts where skiing is offered in Turkey, but not all of them are very well developed. The resorts of interest to expatriates will probably reduce to those listed below, unless you are keen to taste all the options available.

1. Uludağ near Istanbul is the most famous winter resort in Turkey. An easy drive less than an hour from Bursa, the resort is easily accessed from Istanbul for day trips or weekend visits. Though the season is quite short – late December to the end of March – the average

snowfall gives a good covering for skiing. The skiing is
complemented by a number of hotels and well over a dozen
chairlifts and draglifts.

2. Kartalkaya is halfway between the diplomatic capital of Ankara and
   the commercial capital of Istanbul, near the town of Bolu. The
   season and snow quality matches Uludağ, but it can get slightly
   slushy towards the end of the season. There are fewer facilities than
   at Uludag, but the slopes are also less crowded and are more easily
   accessed from Ankara.

3. Elmadağ is only 12 miles from Ankara and is at a lower altitude
   than Uludağ and Kartalkaya, giving less snow and a shorter season.
   The facilities are limited, but some of the universities in Ankara
   have lodges near the ski centre.

4. Mount Erçiyes near Kayseri, is an extinct volcano with north facing
   slopes at a good altitude giving a longer season of almost five
   months. The ski slopes are, however, limited as are the facilities and
   many skiers have to stay miles from the resort in Kayseri due to lack
   of accommodation on Erçiyes itself.

5. Saklıkent is near Antalya, on the mountain of Beydağları. The skiing
   area is at a low altitude and the ski season is very short with only a
   thin covering of snow. The ski facilities and accommodation are
   both limited.

6. Palandöken is near Erzerum at an altitude of over 3,000 metres, with
   good powdery snow giving a five month season. The skiing and the
   facilities are all excellent and can comfortably cater for thousands of
   visitors, with the added option of illuminated evening skiing.

7. Ilgaz Ski Center is at Kastamonu with a good length of slopes,
   though the altitude is not great. The season is four months at the
   most with only a few chairlifts, though the Nordic and cross-country
   skiing is good during this time.

8. Davraz Ski Center is between Isparta and Antalya and, though the
   facilities are limited, the skiing is good. Access from Antalya is easy
   and development of the resort is continuing.

Wine

There is a long history of wine (*şarap*) production in Turkey, dating back thousands of years, and the country is one of the top five producers of grapes in the world. Most of the grapes, however, are eaten in their natural state, or made into raisins.

Modern wine production originates from the early 1920s. TEKEL, originally a French company that was nationalised in 1922 and turned into the state tobacco and alcohol monopoly, produced cigarettes and alcoholic drinks for the mass market. The other leading producer, Kavaklidere, on the other hand was a private family firm that had large agricultural holdings producing grapes. They produced their first batch of wine in 1929.

Mustafa Kemal Atatürk took a liking to Kavaklidere wine and they went from strength to strength. Today, they are the leading wine producer in Turkey and produce a variety of wines to suit all tastes and budgets.

With an excellent climate for growing grapes there are many hundreds of native varieties in Turkey, though not all are commercially productive or suitable for eating or wine making. Most regions of Turkey produce some form of wine, as well as a range of wine vinegars. Both red and white wines are produced, though the quality is hugely variable.

Apart from Kavaklidere, some of the other brands to watch out for are Buzbağ (from Eastern Anatolia), Pammukkale (Denizli), Koçabağ and Turasan (both from Cappadocia) and Chateau Kaleçik. In supermarkets and restaurants the names to look out for in terms of cheaper, but drinkable wines are Kavak, Dikmen, Villa Dolluca, Lâl and Çankaya, which include red, white and rosé varieties.

In Cappadocia the Turasan vineyard runs tours and sells its wine by the case at a discount. Koçabağ have a discount warehouse selling wine by the case that you will have to ask directions for.

Boating

Leisure-related sailing in Turkey is carried out mostly on the Aegean and Mediterranean coasts. The good summer weather, clear seas, stunning coastline and an abundance and variety of boats makes sailing an easy and enjoyable activity. Some of the in-land freshwater lakes host fishing boats, but leisure sailing is not common on these waters.

Day trips, live-aboards, crewed and bare yachts are easily rented and the choice further expands with the option of a traditional Turkish *gulet*, or a standard yacht. RYA sailing courses are also available using dinghies, though many of the charter yachts offer 'informal' instruction during their cruises.

There is an expanding number of dedicated marinas for sailors, but there are also numerous fishing ports where boats can be tied up with the agreement of the local fishermen, or harbourmaster, for a reasonable fee. Marinas are available at Antalya, Finike, Kemer, Kuşadasi, Ayvalik, Istanbul, Ceşme, Izmir, Bodrum, Göçek, and Marmaris, with more than one at Marmaris, Istanbul and Antalya.

Fishing, Hunting and Shooting

Fishing, where it happens, is predominantly a source of food for Turks. There is good sea fishing on all the coasts and Turkey rightly has a good reputation for sea food. Freshwater fishing is also good, with many rivers offering great trout among other species. Some of the larger lakes also provide good fishing, but again this is usually on a commercial basis.

There is no licensing system for fishing in Turkey, but the permission of the landholder may be necessary and fishing is forbidden in certain closed (military) areas.

Hunting is a popular pastime for many Turks, but is also a good source of food for many rural families. A number of species – bear, hook horned mountain goat (*şamua*), wild goat (*bezoar*), wild boar, lynx, wolf, jackal and fox – are designated with permission for hunting, but foreigners can only hunt them in organised parties in designated areas.

The Ministry of Tourism and Culture maintains on its website (www.kultur.gov.tr) a list of tour agencies licensed to run hunting parties and further information can be found in Turkish on the website of the Ministry of Forest, National Parks and Hunt (www.milliparklar.gov.tr).

Turkish Sports

The traditional sports of Turkey date back hundreds of years. The Edirne Oil Wrestling Championship is approaching its 650th anniversary and *jereed* has been in Turkey since around the time the Normans invaded England in 1066AD.

Being limited to Turkey and with a booming tourism industry, the traditional sports competitions have become increasingly commercialised, though no less exciting.

Oil wrestling (*yağli gures*) dates back to the days of the Ottoman Empire and the most famous tournament takes place near Edirne. The wrestlers wear heavy leather trousers and cover themselves in olive oil before trying to up-end each other and dump their opponent on the ground.

Camel wrestling grew out of the natural fighting between camels for dominance in the herd. Historically it occurred throughout Anatolia and the Aegean region, but it is now restricted to the areas around Selcuk, Mugla, Ephesus and Izmir.

Jereed came originally from Selçuks and grew out of the necessary fighting skills of the nomadic warring tribes. The 'game' consists of two opposing teams throwing javelins at each other to try and gain points by hitting an opponent or catching a javelin thrown at him. An exciting, though dangerous game, it is now only played in Eastern Anatolia around Erzurum, Erzincan, Bayburt, Kars and Soğut.

Spa Resorts

The traditional spa resorts of Turkey have grown out of the hot springs that were used to feed the *hammams*. Over time various attributes have been awarded to the various spas, some of which have been backed up by medical analysis.

As a geologically-active area, Turkey is well served by hot springs and other natural, mineral-rich water sources. Some sources are still used to supply small *hammams* in little villages, whilst others have been used to develop huge resort hotel and spa complexes. There are 17 registered spas, though many other facilities operating as *hammams* could lay claim to the title too.

Though the majority are traditional, mineral-rich hot spring spas, the Kangal Sivas Fish Springs is famous for the fact that fish add to the therapeutic properties of the water by nibbling on the skin of bathers who are seeking relief from psoriasis among other skin conditions.

Local recommendation for spas will send you to traditional locations and *hammams*, though if you are looking for the grander experience then opting for the modern resort hotels may be the better option as some of the existing medical spas have received little investment for many years and the facilities are tired. One of the most spectacular is the Kizilçahamam resort hotel in the mountains north of Ankara, with its indoor and outdoor inter-connected pools allowing you to swim under the wall and enjoy the steaming hot water whilst surrounded by snow.

Hammam

A *hammam* is a traditional bathhouse where, for centuries, Turks of all classes went to bathe. They are a blend of differing styles of public baths from the Middle East to northern Europe and date back to Roman times and beyond.

They vary in size from small, single-room facilities in the villages and local neighbourhoods of cities to large municipal facilities. There are hundreds of *hammams* all over the country and some are hundreds of years old and of historical architectural importance. From the grand baths of Istanbul and Ankara to the small buildings in the mountains fed by hot springs, the variety is endless.

There will usually be a hot/steam room where bathers will hang out to chat and socialise as well as wash using the ready supply of hot water. A masseur/masseuse will also be on-hand for a traditional heavy-handed Turkish massage and scouring with oils and scraper.

In some *hammams* built around older Roman facilities there may be a plunge pool; these may be fed by a local hot spring rather than heated water.

The *hammam* is more than just a place to wash. It fulfils a major role in the customs and way of life of most Turks. The bath has been important in the region for centuries, though the practices of the various cultures and religions who bathed have combined over the centuries into the modern practices of today.

They are a social experience and it is well worth joining a group of Turks when attending the baths, so as to enjoy the full cultural experience. Personal recommendation is the best way to find both the grandest architectural *hammams* as well as the truly authentic Turkish experience in the area where you live.

Men and women often use the same facilities, though at different times of day. Whilst the men will always keep themselves covered it is not unusual for the women to go naked, though many will wear underwear or a swimming costume. Only in the modern resort hotels built for foreigners are there mixed facilities.

Caravanning and Camping

Camping is a popular holiday experience for many Turks and there are formal and informal camp-sites dotted around the country, with many right on the foreshore on the Mediterranean, Aegean and Black Sea coasts.

Limited online listings of camp-sites in Turkey can be found on a few websites, though there are many more that can be found by personal recommendation.

11
Health and Social Security

The Turkish social security system and delivery of healthcare provision is well developed, though it is underfunded and very stretched. With the support of the World Bank, the Turkish government has been reviewing the system. It has been introducing reforms to streamline the bureaucracy and introduce efficiency savings to increase the sustainability of the system and improve the quality of the services.

These reforms under way include the merging of parallel pension providers and social security systems under one administration and increasing funding for healthcare provision.

While there is a lot more that can be done to improve the service, the social welfare system is better developed than in many other countries and the healthcare system provides a lifeline to many poorer families who could never afford their own private medical insurance.

TURKISH SOCIAL SECURITY SYSTEM

Subscription to the state-run social security system is compulsory and there are schemes for employees (Social Security Department; Sosyal Güvenlik Kurum) and the self-employed (Sosyal Güvenlik Kurumu Başkanlığı Bağ-Kur).

Both schemes cover healthcare, maternity care, invalidity and work-related injuries as well as providing old age pension and widow(er) benefits. Foreign workers can opt to limit their coverage to the short-term provision which excludes invalidity, old age pension and death.

As mentioned in Chapter 6, employers' contributions to the SSK are 19.5% of salary payments and the employees' contribution is 14%, while self-employed workers contribute 40% of their income. There are minimum and maximum monetary contributions for employees (approx YTL640; YTL4,150) and the self-employed (approx YTL325; YTL1500). In circumstances where the workplace is deemed high risk, the employer's contributions may be increased.

Unemployment payments are covered by an additional contribution of 2% for employers, 1% for employees and a further contribution of 1% from the government.

The social security system and employment are regulated by the Ministry of Labour and Social Security (Çalışma ve Sosyal Güvenlik Bakanlığı).

RECIPROCAL SOCIAL SECURITY AGREEMENTS

Canada

Canada and Turkey have a reciprocal social security agreement that allows contributions paid in one country to be considered in another when calculating old age pension. The agreement is applied if your pension in the country where you are claiming cannot be paid because you have not made enough contributions to the pension plan in that country. Further details for Canadians can be obtained from the Service Canada website (www.servicecanada.gc.ca). Canadians can collect their pension outside of Canada if they lived in Canada for at least 20 years after the age of 18.

UK

There is a social security agreement in place between Turkey and the UK and contributions paid in one country can be taken into consideration when calculating pension in the other.

If you are eligible for a UK pension, then it will be paid in full as if you were living in the UK, even if you reside in Turkey.

Further up-to-date information for UK citizens on living abroad is provided on the website of the Department of Work and Pensions (www. dwp.gov.uk).

Australia, America and New Zealand

There is no reciprocal social security agreement for New Zealanders, Australians and Americans resident in Turkey.

Americans can usually claim their pension whilst living outside of the USA, though in some cases it can only be paid into a US bank account.

Australians can only claim their state pension if they are living in Australia or one of 18 other countries. However, Turkey is not one of these and so an Australian state pension cannot be paid to someone whilst they are living in Turkey.

HEALTHCARE SYSTEM

The Turkish state provides a comprehensive public healthcare system for medical treatment available to all Turkish nationals and foreign nationals resident in the country and paying their SSK contributions. Whilst the service is comprehensive and wide ranging, the limited amount of funding available means that the facilities are not always to the standard that many expatriates would hope for.

The medical services themselves are of a high quality, though, and many of the doctors have international qualification and experience to complement their Turkish training. It is not uncommon to find that doctors are bilingual or even trilingual, with German and English the most common languages languages spoken by the medical staff.

The increasing affluence of many Turks and the wealthy international residents has driven demand for private healthcare and the private sector has responded with increased provision. Many of the senior doctors in the state hospitals also operate in the private sector and offer shorter waiting times, for the same quality of treatment, in more luxurious surroundings.

Dental, optical and other services are widely available.

PRIVATE HEALTH SYSTEM

Most expatriate employees are covered by a private health insurance programme and the hospitals available to them under this sort of coverage are of international standard. Even so, these hospitals will not always offer full surgical and specialist services and, on occasions, it may still be necessary to attend public hospitals for treatment of such conditions as cancer, or other specific medical complaints or surgical procedures. Where a specialist does operate in a private capacity they may rent a surgical theatre from a private or public hospital to carry out the procedure.

Maternity specialists, for example, will often run only a clinic, but have an arrangement to use a specific hospital for the actual delivery. In these circumstances the specialist will generally opt to use the best facilities available.

Most embassies will provide a list of doctors who can speak your own language, though personal recommendation is often the most reliable way to find a suitable doctor or specialist that will suit your needs.

If you need to purchase your own private health insurance it is worth considering using a Turkish insurance company as they can be competitively priced. Your home base will then be considered as Turkey, though, and if you want to be repatriated to your home country it may be necessary to purchase worldwide insurance cover from that country.

EMERGENCY MEDICAL CARE

Emergency services at a hospital (*hastane*) are identified by an '*acil*' sign and such facilities will treat all emergencies that arrive, though you will be billed before departure where appropriate.

It is worth identifying the nearest, or best, emergency hospital in your locality and ensuring that your medical insurance will cover you for treatment there. As some of the insurance companies operate their own hospitals (e.g. Bayindir Sigorta) you may well be restricted to using their own medical services if there is a facility within a certain distance of where you are when treatment is required.

In rural areas you would normally expect to attend the nearest medical centre for initial treatment, before being transferred, or sent on, to another hospital for further treatment.

When driving to hospital with someone needing emergency treatment Turkish motorists will wave a white handkerchief, or piece of white cloth, out of the window to signal they want people to move out of the way.

AMBULANCES

An emergency ambulance can be called by dialling 112 from any phone. However, unless your Turkish is passable, then asking for assistance from a Turkish speaker is probably advisable.

Some of the private medical insurance programmes include access to a private ambulance service and keeping the relevant numbers to hand is a sensible precaution. Private ambulance services can also be used on a one-off basis on payment of a suitable fee.

State Hospitals

The hospitals operated by the state health service provide a full range of services and if you are paying your SSK contributions you will be eligible to use the specialist services where necessary. Access to the specialist services is usually by referral from your family doctor, except in the case of emergency. The medical provision in the state hospitals can be of excellent quality, even when the environment leaves something to be desired.

Personal recommendation from friends and acquaintances can be invaluable when choosing whether to use the state health care system or utilise the alternative private medical services.

State hospitals are designated as '*devlet hastanesi*'; some operate as general hospitals while others specialise in areas such as oncology, maternity or surgery.

Private Hospitals and Laboratories

Affluent, professional Turks have driven demand for private medical services and the insurance (*sigorta*) companies have satisfied this demand with numerous medical insurance schemes on offer, and by increasing numbers of private hospitals and laboratories.

Many of the medical staff in the private system also work in the state healthcare sector for the professional recognition it gives them, whilst earning additional income in the private sector.

Some of the more well-known private hospitals and laboratories are listed in Appendix A, but the list is not exhaustive and personal recommendation as well as the restrictions of your medical insurance will determine which will be the best option for for you.

MEDICAL CLINICS

Medical clinics sit somewhere in between a family doctor service and a hospital. Many have nurses in attendance for treating injuries and dressing wounds, while some have x-ray machines and more advanced equipment. In rural areas these clinics can be as well-equipped as the cottage hospitals in the UK used to be.

In rural areas these clinics will be government run and unless you pay your SSK contributions and have your medical card with you, you will have to pay for treatment. When away from home and travelling around the country, local residents will be happy to direct you to the nearest clinic if you are in need of treatment. The clinics are often signposted with the Red

Crescent symbol, 'H' road signs (as for Hospital in many countries), or as *'Hastane'*.

In urban areas, private clinics often specialise in specific services such as x-rays or lab tests and a private doctor may direct you to attend various places to complete any necessary tests for a diagnosis.

Opticians

Opticians (*gözlükçü*) in Turkey operate like their counterparts in Europe and elsewhere, usually offering eye tests, lenses and frames in a variety of different qualities and specifications. Designer frames are as much in demand and as freely available in Turkey as in any other fashion-conscious country. Large pharmacies (*eczane*) will also have opticians operating in their stores.

Where necessary there are also specialist eye doctors for more serious conditions that require medical treatment as opposed to corrective lenses. Your personal doctor, or an optician, will be able to recommend where you should go for any necessary treatment.

Dentist

Most people will happily avoid attending a dentist (*dişçi*), even though they realise that this is probably not a good idea in the long term. There is no excuse not to see a dentist in Turkey as there are many well-qualified and reputable dentists operating throughout the country.

A few medical insurance programmes also include dental treatment, or subsidise it if they do not cover it in full. Fees are variable and can be expensive, so agreeing a price in advance is advisable if you are not to suffer more pain after the treatment when you get the bill.

Pharmacy

Pharmacies (*eczane*) are open long hours from 09:00–19:00, usually for six days a week. Most will be closed on Sunday, but at least one will be open for 24 hours in each area. Every pharmacy displays a notice in its window when closed, which will list the name, address and phone number of the nearest emergency pharmacies (*nöbetçi eczane*).

Thermal Centres

While not normally classed as medical services in many countries, the thermal resorts of Turkey are generally known for specific healing properties. There are numerous hot springs (*kaynarca*) around the country and some are developed medical resorts, with hotels and clinics for visitors. Some have been in operation for thousands of years and resorts with water sources with healing properties are known as healing water (*şifalı su*). If the water is naturally heated they are also known as hot springs (*içme*).

The healing qualities vary with the chemical and mineral content and the temperature of the water. Some of the resorts have open air pools and others are covered. The open air pools of the hot springs can be be visually superb when they are high in the mountains and the snow is covering the ground while you are able to swim in luxuriously warm water.

Some of the resorts are small and there is little more than a simple *hammam* where men and women have set times to use the single facility. Other resorts are modern, international-standard hotels with treatment rooms, medical staff and therapists available to ensure you have the full spa experience.

12
Conclusion

Whether you choose to make Turkey your home for a few months, a number of years, or the rest of your life, the experience is likely to leave a lasting impression on you and your family and the friends and relatives who visit you.

Turkey is a country of surprises and it is likely to exceed social, political and geographical preconceptions.

The people are outgoing, friendly and welcoming. Away from the tourist hotspots where the local businesses cater for northern Europeans on cheap package tours looking for sun, sand and beer, foreign residents are usually embraced by local residents. Frustrations will occur when two cultures clash and misunderstandings occur, but often as not, with a bit of effort and someone to help with a translation, difficult situations can be resolved.

Many middle class Turks are well-travelled, multi-lingual and cosmopolitan, putting monoglot English speakers to shame. However, when this is combined with the sociable nature of the Turks it opens up a wonderful opportunity to become involved in a culture rather than observing it from a distance, which is the case when living in some countries as an expatriate.

International schools in Turkey often have a high number of Turkish students and, indeed, a wide variety of international students. Expatriate children therefore have the chance to broaden their outlook on the world and become multi-lingual themselves through daily contact with Turkish and other international friends.

Turkish democracy is well established and the population is politically aware, both domestically and internationally, to a level that many Britons will find unnerving. In its early years as a republic, Turkey fought for its position in the world against superpowers and immediate neighbours and emerged as a nation with a sense of purpose.

Recognising the need to balance tradition and religion with freedom and democracy, Turkey continues to wrestle with the dilemma and establish a workable compromise. The fact that this is done openly and noisily by the various political and religious groups in society, with the military, the judicial system and foreign governments all adding their comments, makes more subdued EU mandarins nervous and gives foreign newspapers something to write about.

When the debate gets too out of hand, or the system moves too far to the right, left, or to religion, the military will increase the pressure to bring everyone back to the middle ground. Though there have been three military coups in Turkey, when the army took over for short periods of time and quickly organised new elections, crises in the past 20 years have been solved with less dramatic intervention.

Everyone knows that Istanbul is the only city that straddles two continents, but Turkey itself stretches from Europe to the Middle East and the social, cultural, economic, geographical, dietary and political divide is not so conveniently demarcated.

In the east of Turkey there are numerous ethnic groups, whose various languages and cultures date back thousands of years. There are the Laz in the north east near Georgia and the Kurds in the south east near Iraq and Iran, but they differ as much from each other as they do from Thracians in European Turkey along the Greek and Bulgarian borders.

The mosaic of cultures and traditions that persist across Turkey adds local interest to the already hugely different way of life that is part of the Turkish experience. To add a layer to this is the variation in the cuisine that goes with the cultural contrasts.

If proof were needed that fast food need not be unhealthy, Turkey has a lot to teach the world. *Kebabs* are not just the spinning *doner*, or the skewered meat chunks of *shish* predominantly seen in northern Europe. *Tokat kebab* are vegetarian and cooked in great clay ovens. *Iskender kebab* is a full meal of grilled meat that includes salad, bread, yoghurt and a sauce made with a tomato base. Other endless local varieties appear on menus in villages and wayside restaurants all over the country.

Italy is famous for its pizza, but Turkey has its own unique versions. *Lahmaçun* are thin, unleavened plates of dough that are spread with a spicy paste of lamb, onions, chilli and coriander, then traditionally baked in charcoal fired ovens. *Pide* are similar to Indian naan breads, but are used like pizza bases and covered with a variety of toppings and again baked in hot ovens. Restaurants commonly specialise in *lahmaçun* and *pide* and popular eateries will be packed with diners feasting on freshly-cooked platters.

Some regions are well known for producing certain types of food-based businesses. Apart from tea, Rize has also provided large numbers of bakers for the bakeries of Istanbul and other cities. Many patisseries, which sell sweet and sticky cakes so loved by the Turks, are run by families from the east of the country.

The culinary variety is likely to have arisen as a result of the geographical effects on what foodstuffs could be grown by local residents. The coasts had a plentiful supply of fish, but inland there are large tracts of non-arable mountain regions as well as prime agricultural land. The weather also plays a part and it should never be forgotten that while the coasts are temperate, the inland areas can be brutal in their extremes. Temperature variations of 60°C are not uncommon in Ankara, from summer high of 40°C to mid-winter lows of –20°C.

The upshot is that moving to Turkey is likely to be a multicultural experience, giving you the chance to interact with a variety of cultures all contained within one geo-political border.

CASE STUDY

Kirsten Lauer (USA) – Living in Turkey

Upon being invited to describe my life in Turkey, a small dilemma immediately presented itself. Turkey's peoples and cultures are as variegated as the weaves and patterns in a kilim: would any one person's experiences from Ankara provide enough of a view for the reader? Like most other large countries, Turkey has distinct northern, southern, eastern, western, and interior cultures. Economic factors, visible class lines, and a multitude of minority ethnic and religious influences will also affect the visitor's experience, so that it is sometimes difficult to pinpoint a stereotypical existence here. Then, I realised that in some ways Ankara is a fantastic reference point for the visitor, as it is a crossroads between the geographical and cultural aspects that make up Turkey. It was selected to be the capital and diplomatic centre of the Turkish Republic because of this aspect.

When I married my husband in 2002, the entire process brought to light the differences and variety in Turkish culture. Some of my Turkish teacher friends had planned a henna/hen night for me, and we invited my mother-in-law to be. She is a doctor from Istanbul, and as my friends prepared the coins dipped in henna and pressed them into the palms of our hands to leave their print as good luck, she informed us that this was her first henna night. Henna was not a tradition in her family and she was just as much the curious foreigner in this instance as I was. When trying food from a different region of Turkey she is just as amazed as I am when eating something for the first time.

Of course, I also experienced cultural conflicts during the planning and execution of this wedding: nothing here is planned until last minute, and for a bride with long-distance relatives requiring flights for a specific date this was a little tricky to say the least. The upside of this is that when things don't go the way you want them to you learn that that's not necessarily a disaster, and sometimes even a benefit. I guess you could say that you learn to appreciate surprises, which is a very good attribute to have in life.

An obvious demonstration of the mingling of differences here is the way in which women, in particular, choose to dress themselves. While nearly everyone is Islamic, one's particular sect of Islam can be seen in how one dresses. Lack of head scarf, type of head scarf, knotting of headscarf, outer coats, or spaghetti strap tank tops with bare midriffs all say something about the beliefs and status of the person wearing them. It is not uncommon for me to see two girls walking with linked arms, one of them covered from head-to-toe, and the other in a skimpy t-shirt, jeans and platform shoes. In the school where I work it is not unheard of for a teacher to have to remind a high school student of our rather casual dress code when a skirt is too high or too much tummy is showing. In general, no matter the mode of attire or gender, a great deal of emphasis is put on appearance here, and that seems to be a uniting theme amidst all the teeming variety. Hair styles and colours can change monthly, clothes are tailored, brows groomed, and hands manicured. Pride in one's appearance seems to be considered almost a moral prerequisite.

I see myself learning about significant cultural differences again with my son's nanny. It took me a long while to understand her because she drops off the last consonant and sometimes even the last syllable of her words. When she sees that I don't understand her, she raises her voice just to make sure she's all clear with me. This illiterate Bulgarian/Turkish woman from a nearby village has raised two daughters and two grandchildren, and divorced herself from a difficult husband. She lives in a small whitewashed adobe house with a meticulously kept garden in the middle of the city: because of the lack of heating and their architectural instability, these houses – however quaint they may be to us foreigners – are regarded as the height of poverty. When this woman comes to my house she runs vast amounts of water in order to wash all the surfaces off ... despite the fact that Ankara is facing a serious drought. She adds meat to all vegetable dishes because for her, meat is an expensive and valuable item that makes any dish worthwhile, even if it is meant to be a vegetable dish. It is her way of showing that she cares about me. I wouldn't wear slippers in the house, so she knitted me some and brought them in. Apparently, if I don't wear them I will get seriously sick. I am 40, and not sick yet. Also, if I sit on the floor I will not be able to have children. When I pointed out that I have been sitting on floors all my life and had just had a child, she solemnly took that into account with a look of disbelief. As she wraps her cheery headscarves about her head and swaddles herself in yet another pair of pantaloons in order to leave my house this wintry afternoon, I wonder just how warm her wooden stove is at night in the snow.

I also occasionally wonder how my life has got to be where it is now, in Ankara, Turkey, more or less permanently it seems. I first arrived in Ankara 10 years ago. A small plane delivered me from the large, bustling airport in Istanbul to what was then a small, provincial airport with two terminals and smelling distinctly of sheep. My past five years in the Far East were instantly rendered useless as a frame of reference, and as a small mini-van drove me to my new place of work at a suburban university I realised with a small shock that I might very well be in central California for all the rolling, sun kissed hills sprinkled with oak and olive. My new home was a neatly-landscaped, green oasis of peace and good health. This was not necessarily the case downtown or generally reflective of people's lifestyles however. Downtown was generally grey with dust and mostly comprised of concrete. Downtown, the university students did what university students did the world-over; they smoked and drank and danced with a relish and openness that surprised me at the time. Since then, I have learned that caffeine, tobacco, and alcohol are all highly traditional pastimes here.

In ten years, much has changed. Where it was once so difficult and frustrating to find a single bottle of soy sauce, I now have pretty much everything I need to make most kinds of Chinese, Thai, or Indian food. A journey to a large supermarket used to be a truly exciting event. Now, the latest of many enormous shopping malls has recently opened: this one includes a gallery aquarium equipped with sharks, a neo-classical 'floating' dome in the centre with a tiled mosaic of an old world map underneath it, and all the latest trendy international restaurants in an atrium court. All for a price of course, although the great weekend markets are still the best source for some of the tastiest vegetables in the world. Ankara is no longer a cheap place to live, and prices have gone up astronomically as Turkey competes for EU standards.

Ankara has made huge efforts to improve itself as a capital city over the last few years. The tiny two terminal airport I once arrived in is now a sleek, glass, steel and concrete feat of modern architecture with swooping ceilings and sparkling gift shops. A lake has been turned into a public park with a boardwalk, green children's parks, many cafés, and a section devoted to the national obsession of barbecuing. Under the new mayor, street dogs are given vaccinations and tagged and collared to demonstrate their health. During Kurban Bayram, animals are no longer slaughtered in public streets or even in public view. Many new apartment complexes are equipped with fitness trails and walking paths. Last but not least, the post office requires you to see fewer personnel and to receive fewer stamps in order to pick up the packets that concerned relatives send you in case Turkey doesn't have things like bedspreads or noodles.

I remember with some longing the long walks my Turkish husband and I used to take with our dog, climbing hills to avoid flocks of sheep and their donkey-riding shepherds, before construction claimed the land and turned it into pillars of apartments. There was even one occasion, just before Christmas, when while sitting at home that same dog leaped up to our window growling, and I looked up just in time to see one of those shepherds on a donkey, escorted by large kangal herding dogs, herding a flock of … turkeys. Yes, turkeys – these birds are now a New Year item on many plates in Ankara, and that enterprising shepherd in the middle of nowhere was taking his birds in to see if he could make some money off the foreigners at Christmas time as well.

Years later it is again another Christmas. As I write this in a Starbuck's café minutes from my home. I realise that in the ten years that I have been here, nothing has brought me so close to understanding Turkey as marrying my husband and having our son. Our son is just about to turn one at the time of this writing, and he will grow up with two cultures, two passports, and two languages. I can't think of many better starts in life than that.

Appendix A

Please note that all phone and fax numbers have been presented in international format: please delete the country code and add a zero if phoning from within the country concerned.

TURKISH EMBASSIES AND CONSULATES

Turkish Embassy in London, UK – 43 Belgrave Square, London SW1X 8PA; Tel +44 20 7393 0202; Fax +44 20 7393 0066; www.turkishembassylondon.org

Turkish Consulate General in London, UK (for visa applications) – Rutland Lodge, Rutland Gardens, Knightsbridge, London SW7 1BW; Tel +44 20 7591 6900; Fax +44 20 7591 6911; turkishconsulate@btconnect.com; www.turkishconsulate.org.uk

Office of Commercial Counsellor in London, UK – 43 Belgrave Square, London SWIX 8PA; Tel +44 20 7235 4991; Fax +44 20 7235 2207; dtlon@turkishtrade.org.uk; www.turkishtrade.org.uk

Office of the Economic Counsellor in London, UK – Turkish Embassy, 43 Belgrave Square, London SW1X 8PA; Tel +44 20 7235 2743; Fax +44 20 7235 1020; lonekonm@btclick.com; www.turkisheconomy.org.uk

Turkish Embassy in Ottowa, Canada – 197 Wurtemburg Street, Ottawa ON, K1N 8L9; Tel +61 3 789 4044; Fax +61 3 789 3442; www.turkishembassy.com

Turkish Embassy in Canberra, Australia – 6 Moonah Place, Yarralumla, ACT 2600 Canberra; Tel +61 2 6234 0000; Fax +61 2 6273 4402; turkembs@bigpond.net.au; www.turkishembassy.org.au

Turkish Consulate General in Melbourne, Australia – 8th Floor 24 Albert Road, P.O.Box 323, South Melbourne, VIC 3205; Tel +61 3 9696 6066; Fax +61 3 9696 6104; turkcons@bigpond.com

Turkish Consulate General in Sydney, Australia – 66 Ocean Street, P.O.Box 222 Woollahra N.S.W. 2025 Sydney; Tel +61 2 9328 1155; Fax +61 2 9362 4533; bkturk@bigpond.net.au

Turkish Consulate General Commercial Councellor's Office in Melbourne, Australia – 8th Floor 24 Albert Road, South Melbourne VIC 3205; Tel +61 3 9682 5448; Fax +61 3 9682 5449; dtmel@bigblue.net.au; www.counsellors.gov.tr; www.turkishtradeinfo.org.au

Turkish Consulate General Office of the Labour Attaché in Melbourne Australia – 8th Floor 24 Albert Road, South Melbourne VIC 3205; Tel +61 3 9686 7446

Turkish Consulate General Commercial Counsellor's Office in Sydney, Australia – 66 Ocean Street, P.O.Box 222, Woollahra N.S.W. 2025 Sydney; Tel +61 2 9327 6639; Fax +61 2 9362 4730; dtsid@eisa.net.au

Turkish Embassy in Washington, USA – 2525 Massachusetts Avenue, NW, Washington, DC 20008; Tel +1 202 612 6700; Fax +1 202 612 6744; www.turkishembassy.org

Houston, TX. Consulate General (for Alabama, Arkansas, Louisiana, Mississipi, New Mexico, Oklahoma, Tennessee, Texas), 1990 Post Oak Blvd., Suite 1300, Houston, TX 77056; Tel +1 713 622 5849; Fax +1 713 623 6639; turcon@sbcglobal.net; www.trconsulate.org

Los Angeles, CA. Consulate General (for Alaska, Arizona, California, Colorado, Hawaii, Idaho, Montana, Nevada, Oregon, Utah, Washington, Wyoming, Pacific Islands), 6300 Wilshire Blvd. Suite 2010, Los Angeles, CA 90048; Tel +1 323 655 8832; Fax +1 323 655 8681; turkcgla@pacbell.net; www.trconsulate.org

New York, NY. Consulate General (for Connecticut, Delaware, Florida, Georgia, Kentucky, Maine, Massachussetts, New Hampshire, New Jersey, New York, North Carolina, Pennsylvania, Rhode Island, South Carolina, Vermont; Puerto Rico), 821 United

Nations Plaza, New York, NY 10017; Tel +1 212 949 0160;
Fax +1 212 983 1293; tcbkny@broadviewnet.net;
www.trconsulate. org or www.turkishconsulateny.org

Chicago, IL. Consulate General (for Illinois, Indiana, Iowa, Kansas,
Michigan, Minnesota, Missouri, Nebraska, North Dakota, Ohio,
South Dakota, Wisconsin), 360 N. Michigan Avenue, Suite 1405,
Chicago, IL 60601; Tel +1 312 263 0644; Fax +1 312 263 1449;
trchicago@mfa.gov.tr; www.trconsulate.org

Turkish Embassy (New Zealand), 15-17 Murphy Street, Level 8,
Wellington; Tel +64 4472 1290; Fax +64 4472 1277

Turkish Embassy (Belgium), 4 Rue Montoyer, 1000 Bruxelles;
Tel +32 2 513 4095; Fax +32 2 514 0748

Turkish Embassy (Denmark), Rosbaeksvej15, 2100 Copenhagen;
Tel +45 3 920 2788; Fax +45 3 920 5166

Turkish Embassy (France), 16, Avenue de Lamballe, 75016 Paris;
Tel +33 15 392 7112; Fax +33 14 520 4191

Turkish Embassy (Germany), Runge Str. 9 10179 Berlin;
Tel +49 30 275 850; Fax +49 30 275 90 915;
turk.em.berlin@t-online.de; www.tcberlinbe.de

Turkish Embassy (Greece) 8, Vassileos Gheorgiou B Str. 10674,
Athens; Tel +30 1 726 3000; Fax +30 1 722 9597

Turkish Embassy (Ireland), 11 Clyde Road, Ballsbridge, Dublin 4;
Tel +353 1 668 5240; Fax +353 1 668 5014

Turkish Embassy (Italy), Via Palestro 28, 00185 Rome;
Tel +39 6 494 1547; Fax +39 6 494 1526

Turkish Embassy (Russia), 7 Rostovskiy Pereulok 12, Moscow;
Tel +7 95 246 0009; Fax +7 95 245 6348

Turkish Embassy (Saudi Arabia), P.O.Box 94390, Riyadh 11693;
Tel +966 1482 0101; Fax +966 1488 7823

Turkish Embassy (South Africa), 1067 Church Street, Hatfield, 0181
Pretoria; Tel +27 12342 6053; Fax +27 12342 6052

Turkish Embassy (Spain), Calle Rafael Calvo, 18-2 A Y B Madrid 28010; Tel +34 91 319 8064; Fax +34 91 308 6602

Turkish Embassy (Switzerland), Lombachweg, 33 3006 Berne; Tel +41 31 350 7070; Fax +41 31 352 8891; turkembs@bluewin.ch

Turkish Embassy (UAE), Bateen Area West 16 No 143, Abu Dhabi 2; Tel +971 2 665 5421; Fax +971 2 66 2691

EMBASSIES AND CONSULATES IN TURKEY

British Embassy

Ankara, Sehit Ersan Cad No 46/A, Cankaya, Ankara; britembank@fco.gov.uk; Tel +90 312 455 3344; Fax +90 312 455 3353; www.britishembassy.org.tr

British Consulate Generals

Mesrutiyet Cad 34, Tepebasi Beyoglu, 80072, Istanbul; comsec@superonline.com; Tel +90 212 334 6400; Fax +90 212 334 6407

1442 Sokak No 49, PK 300 Izmir; Tel +90 232 463 5151; Fax +90 232 465 0858

British Vice Consulate Antalya, Tel +90 242 244 5313; Fax +90 242 243 2095; comsec@superonline.com

Kibris Sehitleri Caddesi, Konacik Mevkii No 401/B, Bodrum; honconbod@superonline.com; Tel +90 252 319 0093; Fax +90 252 319 0095

Ressam Pefik Bursali, Caddesi No 40, Zemin Kat, 16010 Bursa; Tel +90 224 220 0436; Fax +90 224 220 0331

Cakmak Caddesi, 124 Sokak Mahmut Tece, Is Merkezi A Blok, Kat 4/4, Mersin, c/o Yesil Marmaris Turizm ve Yat Isletmeciligi A.S., Barbaros Caddesi 11, Marina (P.O.Box 8) 48700, Marmaris; brithonmar@superonline.com; Tel +90 252 412 6486/36; Fax +90 252 412 4565

British Honorary Consulate, Fethiye; Tel +90 252 614 6302;
Fax +90 252 614 8394; bhcfethiye@superonline.com

Ireland Embassy

Uğur Mumcu Cad. No 88, MNG Binasi B Blok Kat 3, Ankara 06700;
Tel +90 312 446 6172; Fax +90 312 446 8061;
ireland@superonline.com

Ireland Consulate General

Acisu Sok No 5 D 4, Macka, Istanbul; Tel +90 212 259 6979;
Fax +90 212 259 9815

The Embassy of The United States of America

110 Atatürk Boulevard, Kavaklidere, Ankara 06100;
Tel +90 312 455 5555; Fax +90 312 467 0019;
http://turkey.usembassy.gov

US Consulate Generals

Kaplıcalar Mevkii Sokak No 2, Istinye 34460, Istanbul;
Tel +90 212 335 9000; http://istanbul.usconsulate.gov

Girne Bulvari No 212; Yuregir, Adana; Tel +90 322 346 6262;
Fax +90 322 346 7916; http://adana.usconsulate.gov

Australian Embassy

Uğur Mumcu 88 Kat 7, GaziOsmanPaşa; Tel +90 312 459 9500;
Fax +90 312 446 4827; www.turkey.embassy.gov.au

New Zealand Embassy

Iran Caddesi No 13 K:4, Kavaklidere, Ankara; Tel +90 312 467
9054; Fax +90 312 467 9013; nzembassyankara@ttnet.net.tr

New Zealand Consulate-General:

İnönü Caddesi No 92/3, Taksim, Istanbul; Tel +90 212 244 0272;
Fax +90 212 251 4004; nzhonconist@hatem-law.com.tr;
www.newzealandhc.org.uk

The Canadian Embassy

Cinnah Caddesi No 58, 06690 Cankaya, Ankara; Tel +90 312 409
2712 (consular); Tel +90 312 409 2700; http://geo.international.
gc.ca/canada-europa/turkey/; ankra@international.gc.ca

TURKISH GOVERNMENT DEPARTMENTS AND ORGANISATIONS

Labour and Social Security Ministry (Çalışma ve Sosyal Güvenlik
Bakanlığı), İnönu Boulevard No 42, Eskisehir Yolu, Emek, Ankara,
Tel +90 312 296 6000; Information (Department of Foreigners) +90
312 296 6849; Service (Department of Foreigners) +90 312 296
6851; www.calisma.gov.tr; www.csgb.gov.tr

Social Security Department for Employees (Sosyal Güvenlik
Kurumu); www.ssk.gov.tr

Social Security Department for the Self-employed (Sosyal Güvenlik
Kurumu Başkanlığı Bağ-Kur); www.bagkur.gov.tr

Foreigners work visa department; www.yabancicalismaizni.gov.tr

Turkish Customs Administration (T.C. Başbakanlık Gümrük
Müsteşarlığı); www.gumruk.gov.tr

General Directorate of Revenues (Gelir Idaresi Başkanliği), Ilkadim
Cad. 06450, Dikmen, Ankara; Tel +90 312 415 2900;
Fax +90 312 415 2821; www.gib.gov.tr

Ministry of Foreign Affairs (T.C. Dişişleri Bakanliği), Balgat 06100
Ankara; Tel +90 312 292 1000; www.mfa.gov.tr

Ministry of Justice (T.C. Adalet Bakanliği), 06659 Kizilay, Ankara;
Tel +90 312 417 7770; Fax +90 312 419 3370; www.adalet.gov.tr;

Prime Ministry of Turkey (T.C. Basbakanlik) www.basbakanlik. gov.tr;

Turkish Grand National Assembly (T.C. Büyük Millet Meclisi); www.tbmm.gov.tr;

Presidency of the Republic of Turkey (T.C. Cumhurbaşkanliği); www.cankaya.gov.tr

Ministry of Culture and Tourism (T.C. Kültür ve Turizm Bakanliği), Atatürk Bulvarı No 29, 06050 Opera, Ankara; Tel +90 312 309 0850; Fax +90 312 312 4359; www.kultur.gov.tr

Ministry of the Interior (T.C. İçişleri Bakanliği); www.icisleri.gov.tr

Invest in Turkey; Kavaklidere Mahallesi Akay Caddesi No 5, Cankaya 06640, Ankara; Tel +90 312 413 8900; Fax +90 312 413 8901; www.investinturkey.gov.tr; Overseas contacts: russia@invest. gov.tr; uk@invest.gov.tr; usa@invest.gov.tr; italy@invest.gov.tr; france@invest.gov.tr; germany@invest.gov.tr; gulf@invest.gov.tr

General Directorate of Investments and Enterprises (Yatirim ve Isletmeler Genel Müdürlügü) Ismet Inönü Bulvari No 5, 06100 Emek, Ankara; Tel +90 312 212 8374; Fax +90 312 212 8397; www.kulturturizm.gov.tr; yatirimisletme@kulturturizm.gov.tr.

Undersecretariat of the Treasury (T.C. Başbakanlık Hazine Müsteşarlığı), Inönü Bulvarı No 36, 06510 Emek, Ankara; Tel +90 312 204 6000; www.hazine.gov.tr

Undersecretariat of Foreign Trade (T.C. Başbakanlik Diş Ticaret Müsteşarliği); www.dtm.gov.tr

Directorate General of Insurance, (T.C. Basbakanlik Hazine Müstesarligi), Inönü Bulvari No 36, 06510 Emek, Ankara; Tel +90 312 204 6000; Fax +90 312 212 8871; www.sigortacilik.gov.tr

Ministry of Forest, National Parks and Hunt, Wildlife General Directorate, Ministry of Forest, Gazi Facilities, 11 Nolu Bina Gazi, Ankara; Tel +90 312 221 0879; Fax +90 312 222 5140; www.milliparklar.gov.tr

Association of Turkish Travel Agencies (TURSAB); www.tursab.org.tr

The Turkish Tourism Investors Association (Türkiye Turizm Yatirimcıları Derneği; www.ttyd.org.tr

Federation of Turkish Tourist Guide Associations (Turist Rehberleri Birliği); www.tureb.org.tr

Marmara Region Tourist Hotelkeepers Association (Turistik Otelciler, İşletmeciler ve Yatırımcılar Birliği); www.turob.com

Turkish Radio and Television (TRT); ww.trt.net.tr

Anadolu Agency (Press Agency); www.aa.com.tr

Credit Reference Agency (Kredi Kayit Bürosu); www.kkb.com.tr

Banking Regulation and Supervision Agency (Banlacilik Düzenleme ve Denetleme Kurumu), Atatürk Bulvarı No 191, B Blok, 06680 Kavaklidere, Ankara; Tel +90 312 455 6500; Fax +90 312 424 0877; www.bddk.org.tr

Turkiye Jeotermal Derneği (Turkish Geothermal Association), Hoşdere Cad. No 190/9, Çankaya, Ankara; Tel +90 312 440 4319; Fax +90 312 438 6867; www.jeotermaldernegi.org.tr

Association of the Insurance and Reinsurance Companies of Turkey (Büyükdere St., Büyükdere Plaza No 195, Floor 1-2 34394, Levent, Istanbul; Tel +90 212 324 1950; Fax +90 212 325 6108; genel@tsrsb.org.tr; www.tsrsb.org.tr

Turkey Touring and Automobile Association

Türkiye Turing ve Otomobil Kurumu; www.turing.org.tr/html/teminatlistesieng.htm

Offices issuing Blue Cards

TTOK Head Office; I. Oto Sanayi Sitesi Yanı, 4. Levent, Istanbul; Tel +90 212 282 8140 (ext 4); Fax +90 212 282 8042

Ankara; Gazi Mustafa Kemal Bulvarı Kültür Sk. No 11, Tandoğan; Tel +90 312 229 3806 / 229 3807; Fax +90 312 229 1318

Antalya; Kışla Mah. 47. Sok. Köken Apt. No 5/4; Tel/Fax +90 242 247 0699

Gaziantep; Ali Fuat Cebesoy Bulvarı, Orkide Apt. No 24/A;
Tel +90 342 325 1610; Fax +90 342 325 1611

Izmir; Ali Cetinkaya Bulvarı, Akkaya Apt. No 31/2 Alsancak;
Tel +90 232 421 7149; Fax +90 232 421 3542

Mersin; Mücahitler Cad. No 55 Karadağ İş Hanı 2/10;
Tel +90 324 232 1247; Fax +90 324 232 0492

International Tourist Information Offices

Turkish Culture and Tourism Office, Conseiller D'Information Pres
L'ambassade De Turquie, Rue Monteyer 4 1040, Bruxelles,
Belgium; Tel +32 2513 8230; Fax +32 2511 7951

Turkish Culture and Tourism Office, Bureau Du Tourisme Et
D'Information De Turquie, 102 Av. Des Champs Elysees, 75008
Paris, France; Tel +33 1 456 27868; Fax +33 1 456 38105;
www.infoturquie.com

Turkish Culture and Tourism Office, Informationsabteilung Des
Turkischen, Generalkonsulants Towers, Europa Center 6,0G,
Tauentzien Strasse 9-12, 10789 Berlin; Tel +49 30 214 3752;
Fax +49 30 214 3952; info@tuerkei-kultur-info.de; www.tuerkei-
kultur-info.de

Turkish Culture and Tourism Office, 4th Floor, 29-30 St. James's
Street, London SW1A 1HB; Tel +44 207 839 7778; Fax +44 207
925 1388; info@gototurkey.co.uk; www.gototurkey.co.uk

Turkish Culture and Tourism Office, 5055 Willshire Boulevard
Suite, 850 Los Angeles, California 90036, USA; Tel +1 323 937
8066; Fax +1 323 937 1271; la@tourismturkey.co.uk;
www.tourismturkey.org

Turkish Culture and Tourism Office, Turkish Embassy Information
Counsellor's Office, 821 United Nations Plaza, New York, NY
10017, USA; Tel +1 212 687 2194; Fax +1 212 599 7568;
ny@tourismturkey.org; www.tourismturkey.org

Turkish Embassy Information Counsellor's Office, 2525 Massachusetts
Ave., NW Washington, DC 20008, USA; Tel +1 202 612 6800;
Fax +1 202 319 7446; de@tourismturkey.org; www.tourismturkey.org

Turkish Culture and Tourism Office, Dubai World Trade Center
Bldg, 8th Floor, P.O.Box: 9221 Dubai, UAE;
Tel +971 433 186 6263; Fax +971 433 17317

UTILITIES PROVIDERS

Telephone

Türk Telecom: www.turktelekom.com.tr/eng_default.asp

Internet

Netone (for business customers), Büyükdere Cad. No 121, Ercan
Han Kat 2, 34394 Gayrettepe, Istanbul; Tel +90 212 355 1718;
Fax +90 212 216 5566; sales@netone.net.tr; www.netone.com.tr

E-Kolay: www.e-kolay.net

Superonline: www.superonline.com

Turk.Net: www.turk.net

Mobile phone service providers

Avea: www.avea.com.tr/index_en.shtml

Turkcell: www.turkcell.com.tr/en

Vodafone: www.vodafone.com.tr

COURIER SERVICES

Turkish Bus Company Courier Services

Varan; www.varan.com.tr/english/varan_kargo.asp

Ulusoy; www.ulusoy.com.tr/eng/

International couriers operating in Turkey

UPS Turkey, Ambarlar Caddesi 6/A Blok, 34786 Zeytinburnu,
Istanbul; Customer Service Tel (within Turkey) 444 00 33;
crm@ups.com.tr; Tel +90 212 413 2222; Fax +90 212 414 0200

TNT Turkey: Istanbul Yolu 14 Km., Fatih Sultan Mehmet Bulvarı No 466/A, Ankara; Tel +90 312 255 8383; Fax +90 312 256 3056; Ertürk Sok., Uzka İş Merkezi No 9, Kavacık 34810, Istanbul; Tel +90 216 425 1730; Fax +90 216 425 1710; Customer Service Tel (within Turkey) 444 0 868; www.tnt.com

DHL Turkey: Anakara (Cinnah Front Office), Cinnah Cad. No 38 Çankaya, Ankara; Tel +90 312 441 8744; Fax +90 312 441 8412: Istanbul (Taksim Front Office), Cumhuriyet Cad., Gezi Dükkanları No 20, 80090 Taksim, Istanbul; Tel +90 212 478 1000; Customer Service Tel 444 00 40; Fax +90 212 249 6220; www.dhl.com.tr

TURKISH LANGUAGE SELF STUDY BOOKS

For Children

Ece Ve Efe Ile Turkce (Turkish with Ece and Efe) by Fatih Erdoğan; Milet Publishing; ISBN-10: 1840594934

Milet Flashwords by Sedat Turhan; Milet Publishing Ltd; ISBN-10: 1840594195

For Adults

Turkish Phrasebook; Rough Guides Ltd; ISBN-10: 1843536471

Turkish; Lonely Planet Publications; ISBN-10: 1864503165

Starting Turkish by Orhan Doğan; Milet Publishing Ltd; ISBN-10: 1840594977

Colloquial Turkish: The Complete Course for Beginners by Sinan Bayraktaroglu; Routledge; ISBN-10: 0415157463

CDs

Linguaphone PDQ Turkish; Linguaphone; ISBN-10: 0747308705

Teach Yourself Turkish (Book and CD Pack) by David Pollard; Teach Yourself Books; ISBN-10: 0340871059

Teach Yourself Turkish Conversation (Audio CD) by Sultan Erdoğan; Teach Yourself Books; ISBN-10: 0340927771

Learn to Speak Turkish with Perfect Recall (2 CDs & book); Perfect Recall Systems; ASIN: B000MV82JS

CD-ROM

Talk Now! Learn Turkish; EuroTalk Limited; ASIN: 1843520168

100 Beginner: Turkish; Strokes International; ASIN: 3708702891

Rosetta Stone Level 1 Turkish; www.RosettaStone.co.uk

Online

www.turkish-center.com – Ankara University

www.onlineturkish.com

www.turkishlanguage.co.uk

www.turkishclass.com

http://cali.arizona.edu/maxnet/tur/ – University of Arizona

CLASSROOM TURKISH LANGUAGE COURSES

Outside Turkey

Transglobal Language and Cultures, Merchants Court, Borough Road, Altrincham, Cheshire, WA15 9RA, UK; Tel +44 161 233 0888; www.transgloballanguages.co.uk

International Language Institute, 1337 Connecticut Ave, NW, 4th Floor, Washington, DC 20036; Tel +1 202 362 2505; www.transemantics.com

Cactus Language Training; Suite 34, Eighth Floor, 440 Ninth Avenue, New York NY 10001; Toll Free 1 888 270 3949; www.cactuslanguagetraining.com. Also UK offices at: Marsham Street, London SW1P 3DW and Suite 4, Clarence House, 30-31 North St., Brighton BN1 1EB, East Sussex, UK

In Turkey

Turkish – American Association, Cinnah Caddesi 20, Kavaklidere, Ankara; Tel +90 312 426 3727; Fax +90 312 468 2538; http://www.taa-ankara.org.tr

The EF Turkish Centre, Aydin Sok. F.Block. No 12, 1.Levent, Istanbul; Tel +90 212 282 9064; www.turkishlesson.com

Dilmer Language Centre, İnönü Cadesi, Prof. Tank Zafer Tunaya Sokak No 18 34437 Taksim, Istanbul; Tel +90 212 292 9696; www.dilmer.com

TOMER, Ankara University, GMK Bulvarı No 84, 06570 Maltepe, Ankara; Tel +90 312 232 6634; www.tomer.ankara.edu.tr/english/

EDUCATION

Schools in Turkey Sponsored by Diplomatic Missions

Alman Lisesi – Deutsche Schule, Istanbul (Germany)

Lycée Charles De Gaulle, Ankara (France)

Lycée de Galatasaray, Istanbul (France)

Lycée Francais Saint-Benoît, Istanbul (France)

Oesterreichisches St. Georgs-Kolleg, Istanbul (Austria)

British Embassy Study Group^, Ankara (UK)

Pakistan Embassy Study Group, Ankara (Pakistan)

IBO Schools

Aka Schools^, Basin Sitesi Mah, Radyum Sok. No 21, Bahcelievler, Istanbul; Tel +90 212 557 2772; www.akakoleji.k12.tr

American Collegiate Institute^, Inonu Caddesi, No 476, 35290 Goztepe, Izmir; Tel +90 232 285 3401; www.aci.k12.tr

Ar-El Primary School, Günesli Yolu Atatürk Caddesi, Radar Karsisi, Yenibosna, Bahçelievler, 34530 Istanbul; Tel +90 212 550 4930; www.ar-el.k12.tr

Bilkent University Preparatory School*^, East Campus, 06533 Ankara; Tel +90 312 290 5361; www.bups.bilkent.edu.tr

British International School, Dilhayat Sokak 18, Etiler, Istanbul, Tel +90 212 202 7971; www.bis.k12.tr

Dogus Schools^, Zeamet Sokak No 17, Acibadem, Kadiköy, Istanbul; Tel +90 216 428 7121; www.dogus.k12.tr

Enka Schools^, Sadi Gulcelik Spor Sitesi, Istinye, 34460 Istanbul; Tel +90 212 276 0545; http://enkaschools.com

Eyüboglu High School^, Namik Kemal mah., Dr. Rüstem Eyüboglu sok.3, Ümraniye, Istanbul; Tel +90 216 522 1212; www.eyuboglu.com

Istanbul International Community School*^, Karaagac Koyu, Hadimkoy, Istanbul; Tel +90 212 857 8264; www.iics-k12.com

Istanbul Prof. Dr. Mümtaz Turhan Sosyal Bilimler Lisesi, Fevzi Çakmak Cad. Fatih Mah., No 2 Yenibosna, Bahçelievler, Istanbul; Tel +90 212 551 6146; www.isbl.k12.tr

Koç School^, P.O.Box 60, Tuzla, Istanbul, Istanbul; Tel +90 216 585 6248; www.kocschool.k12.tr

Kultur 2000 College, Alkent 2000, Faz Yani, Karaagaç Yolu, Buyukçekmece, Istanbul; Tel +90 212 857 8466; www.kultur2000.k12.tr

Kultur High School, Incirli Yolbasi Sok. No 1, Bakirkoy, Istanbul; Tel +90 212 570 5444; www.kultur.k12.tr

MEF International School, Ulus Mahallesi, Dereboyu Cad., Ortakoy, Istanbul; Tel +90 212 287 6900; www.mefinternationalschools.com

MEF International School**, Akçay Cd. No 285 Gaziemir, İzmir; Tel +90 232 252 2052; www.mefinternationalschools.com

Marmara Education Group, Marmara Eğitim Köyü 34857 Maltepe, Istanbul; Tel +90 216 626 1000; www.mek.k12.tr

Ozel Kültür Ilkogretim Okulu, 9-10 Kisim, Atakoy, Istanbul; Tel +90 212 559 0488; www.kultur.k12.tr

Private YUCE Schools, YUCE High School, Ozel YUCE Okullari, Zuhtu Tigrel Caddesi, Ismet Eker Sokak No 5, Oran, 06450 Ankara; Tel +90 312 490 0202; www.yuce.k12.tr

Privatschule Der Deutschen Botschaft Ankara, Tunus Cad.56, Cankaya, Ankara; Tel +90 312 426 6382; http://schulwebs1.dasan.de/ds_ankara/

TED Ankara College Foundation High School^, Golbasi Taspinar Koyu Yumrubel Mevkii No 310, Ankara; Tel +90 312 586 9064; www.tedankara.k12.tr

TED Bursa College, 21 Yüzyil Caddesi Mürsel, Köyü Mevkii, Bademli, Bursa; Tel +90 224 549 2100; www.tedbursa.k12.tr

TEV Inanc Turkes High School For Gifted Students, Muallimkoy Mevkii, PK. 125, Gebze, Kocaeli; Tel +90 262 759 1195; www.tevitol.k12.tr

Tarsus American School, Cengiz Topel Caddesi, Caminur Mahallesi 201 Sokak No 64, 33401 Tarsus, Mersin; Tel +90 324 613 5402; www.tac.k12.tr

Yuzyil Isil High School^, Bahçeköy Valide Sultan Cd., Alay Yolu No 2, Sariyer, 34473 Istanbul; Tel +90 212 226 2353; www.yuzyilisil.k12.tr

* NEASC (www.neasc.org) registered school
** NEASC candidate school
^ECIS (www.ecis.org) registered school

Turkish State Funded Universities

Abant Izzet Baysal University; Adnan Menderes University; Afyon Koçatepe University; Akdeniz University; Anadolu University; Ankara University; Atatürk University; Balikesir University; Boğaziçi University; Celal Bayar University; Cumhuriyet University; Canakkale Onsekiz Mart Cukurova University; Dicle University; Dokuz Eylül University; Dumlupinar University; Ege University; Erçiyes University; Firat University; Galatasaray University; Gazi University; Gaziantep University; Gaziosmanpaşa University; Gebze Institute of Technology University; Haçettepe University; Harran University; Inönü University; Istanbul University; Istanbul Technical University; Izmir Institute of Technology University; Kafkas University; Kahramanmaras Sütcü Imam University; Karadeniz Technical University; Kirikkale University; Koçaeli University; Marmara University; Mersin University; Mimar Sinan University; Mustafa Kemal University; Muğla University; Niğde

University; Ondokuz Mayis University; Middle East Technical University (METU); Osmangazi University; Pamukkale University; Sakarya University; Selçuk University; Süleyman Demirel University; Trakya University; Yildiz Technical University; Uludağ University; Yüzüncü Yil University; Zonguldak Karaelmas University

Privately Funded (Foundation) Universities in Turkey

Atilim University; Bahçeşehir University; Başkent University; Beykent University; Bilkent University; Çağ University; Çankaya University; Doğus University; Fatih University; Haliç University; Işik University; Istanbul Bilgi University; Istanbul Commerce University; Izmir Economic University; Kadir Has University; Koç University; Istanbul Kültür University; Maltepe University; Okan University; Sabançı University; TOBB Economic and Technology University; Ufuk University; Yaşar University; Yeditepe University

Distance Learning Resources

The Open University (Student Registration & Enquiry Service, The Open University, P.O.Box 197, Milton Keynes MK7 6BJ, United Kingdom; Tel +44 845 300 6090; Fax +44 1908 654914; general-enquiries@open.ac.uk; www.open.ac.uk) in the UK runs a wide range of courses leading to degree level qualification.

The Regent Academy (Lyne Akres, Brandis Corner, Devon EX22 7YH; Tel +44 1409 220 415; Fax +44 1409 220 416; info@regentacademy.com; www.regentacademy.com) runs a variety of Art and Writing Related Courses and is accredited by City and Guilds as well as the ODLA.

Petersons (Princeton Pike Corporate Center, 2000 Lenox Drive, P.O.Box 67005, Lawrenceville, NJ 08648; Tel +1 609 896 1800; www.petersons.com) educational resources is a useful source of information on education in the US, including distance learning courses.

Cultural Training Providers

Communicaid (London, Frankfurt, Paris & New York); www.communicaid.com

Kwintessential Ltd, 24 Compton Rd, South Petherton, Somerset, TA13 5EN, UK; Tel. +44 845 124 9615; www.kwintessential.co.uk

Culturewise Ltd., Fourth Floor, 16-18 Marshalsea Road, London, SE1 1HL, UK; Tel +44 20 7403 9525; www.transgloballanguages. co.uk

Farnham Castle Intercultural Training; Farnham Castle, Castle Street, Farnham, Surrey GU9 0AG, UK; Tel +44 125 272 0418; www.intercultural-training.co.uk

Language Training Center, 5750 Castle Creek Parkway Suite 387, Indianapolis, IN, 46250, USA; Tel +1 317 578 4577; www.languagetrainingcenter.com

Intercultural Insights, 5420 Delor Street, St. Louis Missouri 63109, USA; Tel +1 314 457 9643; www.interculturalinsights.com

TURKISH MEDIA

Newspapers

Turkish Daily News: www.turkishdailynews.com.tr

Today's Zaman: www.todayszaman.com

The Turkish Herald: www.theturkishherald.com

Hurriyet: www.hurriyet.com.tr/english/

Didim Today: www.didimtoday.com

Turkish Riviera News: http://turkishrivieranews.com

Voices Newspaper: www.voicesnewspaper.com

Satellite TV

TurkSat: www.turksat.com.tr

Digiturk: www.digiturk.gen.tr

RECRUITMENT

EFL Agencies and Employers

International House (UK & worldwide): www.ihworld.com

The International TEFL Corporation (USA): www.teflcorp.com

Saxon Court (UK, NZ, RSA): www.saxoncourt.com

TEFL.com (UK): www.tefl.com

EL Gazete (UK): www.elgazette.com

International Teacher Recruitment Agencies

Teachers International Consultancy (UK): www.ticrecruitment.com

International School Recruitment (UK):
www.internationalschoolrecruitment.com

Teacher Recruitment International (Australia): www.triaust.com

International Teachers Network (UK): www.itnmark.com

Search Associates (UK): www.search-associates.co.uk

Search Associates (UK – Harry Deelman): www.search-associates.net

Search Associates (USA): www.search-associates.com

International Schools Services (USA): www.iss.edu

Education Overseas (USA): www.educatorsoverseas.com

Carney Sandoe (USA): www.carneysandoe.com

University Job Advertisers

Times Higher Education Supplement: www.thesjobs.co.uk

Academic Jobs EU (Europe): http://academicjobseu.com

General Recruitment Websites

Turkey Job Link: www.turkeyjoblink.com

Expat Network: www.expatnetwork.com

Potential Sources of Employers

British Chamber of Commerce in Turkey, Mesrutiyet Caddesi, 18, Asli Han, Kat 6 Galatasaray, 80050 Istanbul; Tel + 90 212 249 0420 /249 0658; Fax + 90 212 252 5551; www.bcct.org.tr

Turkish British Chamber of Commerce and Industry, 2nd Floor Bury House, Bury Street, London SW1Y 6AU; Tel +44 20 7321 0999; Fax +44 20 7321 0989; www.tbcci.org

Turkish US Business Council (Türk Amerikan Iş Konseyi), Dis Ekonomik Iliskiler Kurulu, TOBB Plaza, Talatpasa cad. No 3 Kat:5, 34394 Gultepe, Levent, Istanbul; Tel +90 212 339 5000; Fax +90 212 270 3592; www.turkey-now.org

Association of Turkey's Industrialists and Businessmen (TÜSIAD), Mesrutiyet Cad. No 74, Tepebasi, 34420 Istanbul, Turkey; Tel +90 212 249 5448/249 1929; Fax +90 212 293 3783; www.tusiad.org.tr

Association of Independent Industrialists and Businessmen (MÜSIAD), Mecidiye Cad. No 7/50, Mecidiyeköy, 34387 Istanbul, Turkey; Tel +90 212 213 6100; Fax +90 212 213 7890/216 0142; www.musiad.org.tr

Foreign Investors Association of Turkey (YASED): www.yased.org.tr

International Freight Forwarders' Association of Turkey (UTIKAD), Hürriyet Cd. Bakis Sok. No 8, Kaytaz Villa A-Blok D.1, 34153 Senlikköy, Florya, Istanbul, Turkey; Tel +90 212 599 8484; Fax +90 212 599 9821; www.utikad.org.tr

Turkish Contractors Association, (Türkiye Müteahhitler Birligi), Ahmet Mithat Efendi Sokak 21, Çankaya, Ankara, Turkey; Tel +90 312 440 8122; Fax +90 312 440 0253; www.tmb.org.tr

The Union of Chambers and Commodity Exchanges of Turkey (TOBB); www.tobb.org.tr

Istanbul Chamber of Commerce; Resadiye Cad. 34112 Eminonu; Tel +90 212 455 6000; Fax +90 212 513 1565; www.ito.org.tr

Istanbul Chamber of Industry; Meşrutiyet Cad. No 62, 34430 Tepebaşı, Istanbul; Tel +90 212 252 2900; Fax +90 212 249 5084; www.iso.org.tr

Ankara Chamber of Commerce; Odası Mithatpaşa Cad 62/18, Kızılay, Ankara; Tel +90 312 418 8700; www.ato.org.tr

Ankara Chamber of Industry; Çetin Emeç Bulvarı, 4. Cd. 71. Sk. No 11, Öveçler, Ankara; +90 312 417 1200; Fax +90 312 417 5205; www.aso.org.tr

Izmir Chamber of Commerce; Atatürk Cad. No 126, 35210 Pasaport, Izmir; Tel +90 232 441 7777; Fax +90 232 446 2251; www.izto.org.tr

Aegean Chamber of Industry; Cumhuriyet Bulvarı No 63, Izmir; Tel +90 232 455 2900; Fax +90 232 483 9937; www.ebso.org.tr

Bursa Chamber of Commerce and Industry; Organize Sanayi Bölgesi Mavi, Cadde 2. Sokak No 2, 16159 Nilüfer, Bursa; Tel +90 224 243 1500; +90 224 242 8511; www.btso.org.tr

Kütahya Chamber of Commerce and Industry; Kütahya Ticaret ve Snayi Odasi, Hükümet Cad No 1/3, Kütahya; Tel +90 274 216 1074; Fax +90 274 216 1404; www.kutso.org.tr

Turkey Business Guide, Telmar Iletişim Sistemleri Ltd, Perpa Ticaret Merkezi, B Blok Kat:12 No 2239, Okmeydanı, Istanbul; Tel +90 212 222 7200; Fax +90 212 222 7203: www.turkindex.com

B2B Centre of Turkey; Tel +90 216 418 8000; Fax +90 216 414 5504; www.turksanayi.com

VOLUNTEER ORGANISATIONS

United Planet, 11 Arlington Street, Boston MA, 02116 USA; Tel +1 617 267 7763; Toll-free (US only) +1 800 292 2316; Fax +1 617 267 7764; www.unitedplanet.org

Canadian Alliance for Development Initiatives and Projects, 129-1271 Howe Street, Vancouver, British Columbia, V6Z 1R3, Canada; Tel +1 604 628 7400; Fax +1 604 628 7401; http://cadip.org

World Volunteer Web, United Nations Volunteers, Hermann Ehlers Strasse 10, 53113 Bonn, Germany; Tel +49 228 815 2000; Fax +49 228 815 2001; www.worldvolunteerweb.org

UNA Exchange, Temple of Peace, Cathays Park, Cardiff CF10 3AP, Wales, UK; Tel +44 2920 223088; Fax +90 2920 222540; www.unaexchange.org

Gençlik Servisler Merkeze (Youth Services Centre), Bayındır Sokak. 45/9, Kızılay 06650, Ankara; Tel +90 312 417 1124; Fax +90 312 425 8192; www.gsm-youth.org

Gençtur, Istiklal Cad. No 108, Aznavur Pasajı Kat: 5, 34430 Galatasaray, Istanbul; Tel +90 212 244 6230; Fax +90 212 244 6233; www.genctur.com

4 International Careers & Jobs, 11/16-20 Winchester Street, Carlton, 2218, NSW, Australia; www.4icj.com

EIL, 287 Worcester Road, Malvern, Worcester. WR14 1AB, UK; Tel +44 168 456 2577; Fax +44 168 456 2212; www.overseasvolunteering.co.uk

BUSINESS

Useful Contacts

Istanbul Chamber of Commerce (ITO), Ticari Dokumantasuon Subesi, Resadiye Caddesi, 34378 Eminonu, Istanbul; Tel +90 212 455 6000; Fax +90 212 520 1027; www.ito.org.tr

Istanbul Chamber of Industry (ISO), Mesrutiyet Caddesi No 118, Beyoglu, 80050 Istanbul; Tel +90 212 252 2900; Fax +90 212 249 3963; www.iso.org.tr

Aegean Region Chamber of Industry (EBSO), Cumhuriyet Bulvari No 63, Pasaport, Izmir; Tel +90 232 484 4330; Fax +90 232 483 9937; www.ebso.org.tr

Konya Chamber of Industry; 1 Organize Sanayi Bol. İstikamet Cd. 42300, Konya; Tel +90 332 251 0670; Fax +90 332 248 9351; www.kso.org.tr

Izmir Chamber of Commerce (IZTO), Atatürk Caddesi No 126, Pasaport, Izmir; Tel +90 232 441 7777; Fax +90 232 483 7836; www.izto.org.tr

Ankara Chamber of Commerce (ATO), ATO Sarayi Eskişehir Yolu, Soğutozu, Ankara; Tel +90 312 285 7950; Fax +90 312 286 3446; www.ato-acc.org.tr

Ankara Chamber of Industry (ASO), Atatürk Bulvari 193, Kavaklidere, Ankara; Tel +90 312 417 1200; Fax +90 312 417 2060; www.aso.org.tr

National Franchising Association (Ulusal Franchising Dernegi – UFRAD), Ergenekon Caddesi, Pangalti Is Merkezi 89/15, 80240 Pangalti, Istanbul; Tel +90 212 296 6628; Fax +90 212 224 5130; www.ufrad.org.tr

International Franchising Association, 1350 New York Avenue, NW, Washington DC 20005-4709; Tel +1 202 628 8000; Fax +1 202 628 0812; www.franchise.org

British Franchise Association, Thames View, Newtown Road, Henley-on-Thames, Oxon, RG9 1HG, UK; Tel +44 149 157 8050; Fax +44 149 157 3517; www.thebfa.org

Regus Office Services;
Istanbul – Ayazaga Mah. Meydan Sok. No 28 Beybi Giz Plaza Kat:26 & 27 Maslak, Istabul; Tel +90 212 335 2525; Fax +90 212 335 2500:
Ankara – Armada Shopping and Trade Centre, Floors 11-12, Eskisehir Yolu No 6, Sogutozu, Ankara 06520; Tel +90 312 295 6262; Fax +90 312 295 6200; www.regus.com.tr

Turkish Trade Associations

Foreign Trade Association of Turkey, Kore Sehitleri Caddesi Arcil Apartment No 37/4, Zincirlikuyu, Istanbul; Tel +90 212 272 6981; Fax +90 212 275 5136; www.turktrade.org.tr

Automotive Industrialists Association (OSD), Atilla Sokak No 8, Uskudat-Altunizade, 81190 Istanbul; Tel +90 216 321 4743; Fax +90 216 321 9497; www.osd.org.tr

Association of Automotive Parts Manufacturers (TAYSAD), Organize Sanayi Bölgesi, 41480, Sekerpınar, Gebze, Kocaeli ; Tel +90 262 658 9818; Fax + 90 262 658 9839; www.taysad.org.tr

Association of Electromechanical Industries (EMSAD), Ziyabey
Cad. Dostlar Sitesi, B Blok Kat: 8 D: 83, Balgat, Ankara;
Tel +90 312 284 4032; Fax +90 312 287 3765; www.emsad.org.tr

Ceramic and Refractory Manufacturers Association, Büyükdere
Caddesi No 151 B/31, Zinçirlikuyu, 80300 Istanbul; Tel +90 212
266 4467; Fax +90 212 211 0503; www.turkishceramics.com

The General Secretariat of Istanbul Textile and Apparel Exporter
Associations, Cobancesme Mevkii, Sanayi Cad. Dis Tic. Kompleksi
B-Blok Yenibosna, Bahçelievler, Istanbul; Tel +90 212 454 0200;
Fax +90 212 454 0201; www.itkib.org.tr

Free Trade Zones

Adana Free Trade Zone, P.K.10, 01920 Ceyhan, Adana;
Tel +90 322 634 2080; Fax +90 322 634 2071

Aegean Free Trade Zone, Akcay Caddessi No 144/1, Gaziemir,
Izmir; Tel +90 232 251 0244; Fax +90 232 251 1662

Antalya Free Trade Zone, P.O.Box 650, Yeniliman, 07135 Antalya;
Tel +90 242 259 0188; Fax +90 242 259 0934; www.ant-free-
zone.org.tr

Atatürk Airport Free Trade Zone Havalimani Yesilköy. 34830
Istanbul; Tel +90 212 465 0065; Fax +90 212 465 0068

Bursa Free Trade Zone, P.O.Box 35, Gemlik, Bursa;
Tel +90 224 524 8787; Fax +90 224 524 8788

Denizli Free Trade Zone, P.O.Box 30, 20350 Çardak, Denizli;
Tel +90 258 851 1119; Fax +90 258 851 1038

Erzerum – Eastern Anatolia Free Trade Zone, 25 Temmuz Fuar
Alani, 25050 Erzerum; Tel +90 442 235 2530; Fax +90 442 235
2852

Europe Free Trade Zone, P.O.Box 350, 59860 Çorlu, Tekirdağ;
Tel +90 282 691 1054; Fax +90 282 691 1059; www.asb.com.tr

Gaziantep Free Trade Zone, P.O.Box 1160, Başpinar Mevkii, 27120
Gaziantep; Tel +90 342 359 1031; Fax +90 342 359 1035;
www.freezone-antep.gov.tr

Istanbul Leather and Industry Free Trade Zone, Aydinli-Orhanli Mevkii, 81464 Tuzla, Istanbul; Tel +90 216 394 2128; Fax +90 216 394 1253

Istanbul Thrace Free Trade Zone, Karatoprak Mevkii Nato Karsisi Ferhatpaşa Mahallesi, Çatalca, Istanbul; Tel +90 212 789 2933; Fax +90 212 789 6022

Izmir Menemen Leather Free Trade Zone, Maltepe Köyü, Panaz Mevkii, Menemen, Izmir; Tel +90 232 842 6627; Fax +90 232 842 6347

Kayseri Free Trade Zone, P.O.Box 105, Kayseri; Tel +90 352 311 3981; Fax +90 352 311 3982

Kocaeli Free Trade Zone, Yeni Köy Arpali Mevkii, P.O.Box 33, Gölcük, Kocaeli; Tel +90 262 341 3841; Fax +90 262 341 3821

Mardin Free Trade Zone, Organize Sanayi Bölgesi, 47060 Istasyon, Mardin; Tel +90 482 215 2070; Fax +90 482 215 1517

Mersin Free Trade Zone, P.O.Box 15, Mersin; Tel +90 324 238 7594; Fax +90 324 238 7598

Rize Free Trade Zone, Engindere Mahallesi, Küçük Sanayi Sitesi Yani, 53100 Rize; Tel +90 464 226 0952; Fax +90 464 226 0956

Samsun Free Trade Zone, 55100 Limaniçi, Samsun; Tel +90 362 445 1996; Fax +90 362 445 1108

Trabzon Free Trade Zone, 61100 Liman, Trabzon; Tel +90 462 326 4233 (2 lines); Fax +90 462 326 4235

TÜBITAK MAM Technology Free Trade Zone, P.O.Box 21, 41470 Gebze, Kocaeli; Tel +90 262 646 5371; Fax +90 262 644 3045

Technology Development Zones

Ankara Cyberpark, Cyberplaza Block B, Floor 1, Bilkent 06800 Ankara; Tel +90 312 265 0040; Fax +90 312 265 0048; www.cyberpark.com.tr

Ari Teknokent, ITÜ Ayazaga Kampüsü, Otomasyon Binasi Kat:4, 34469 Maslak, Istanbul; Tel +90 212 285 0789/0817; Fax +90 212 285 0817; www.teknokent.itu.edu.tr

Eskisehir TDF, Anadolu Teknoloji Arastirma Parki A.S., Eskisehir Organize Sanayi Bölge Müdürlügü Binasi Organize Sanayi Bölgesi 2, Cad. 26110 Eskisehir; Tel +90 222 236 0360; Fax +90 222 236 0129; www.atap.com.tr

GOSB Teknopark A.S., Gebze Organize Sanayi Bölgesi, Kemal Nehrozoglu Caddesi, 41480 Gebze, Kocaeli; Tel +90 262 648 4848 (ext: 4846); Fax +90 262 648 4822; www.gosbteknopark.com

Hacettepe University TDZ, Hacettepe University, Beytepe Campus Rector's Building 11th Floor, Beytepe, Ankara; Tel +90 312 297 7162; Fax +90 312 297 7163; www.hacettepeteknokent.com.tr

Izmir TDZ, Izmir Teknoloji Gelistirme Bölgesi A.S., Iyte Campus, Gülbahçe, Urla 35430, Izmir; Tel +90 232 750 6238; Fax +90 232 750 6015; www.iztekgeb.iyte.edu.tr

Kocaeli University TDF, Kocaeli Üniversitesi Teknoloji Gelistirme Bölgesi, Yeniköy, Kocaeli; www.teknopark.kou.edu.tr

Middle East Technical University TDF, Teknopark AŞ, ODTU Teknokent, Orta Dogu Teknik Üniversitesi Kampüsü, Eskisehir Yolu, Ankara; www.metutech.metu.edu.tr

Selçuk University TDF, Selçuk Üniversitesi, Alaaddin Keykubat Kampüsü, Teknokent Binasi, 42070 Selçuklu, Konya; Tel +90 332 241 5455; Fax + 90 332 241 5457; www.konyateknokent.com

TÜBITAK Marmara Research Center TDZ, TÜBITAK-MRC Campus, 41470 Gebze, Kocaeli; Tel +90 262 646 3045; www.mam.gov.tr

Yildiz Technical University TDZ, Yildiz Teknik Üniversitesi Davutpasa Kampüsü, Davutpasa Mah., Davutpasa Caddesi, 34220 Esenler, Istanbul; Tel +90 212 449 1500; Fax +90 212 449 1514; www.yildiz.edu.tr

Organised Industrial Zones (OIZ)

Afyonkarahisar OIZ, Organize Sanayi Bölgesi Müdürlüğü, P.O.Box 6, Afyon; Tel +90 272 221 1465; Fax +90 272 221 1467; www.afyontso.org

Ostim (Ankara) OIZ, Ostim Organize Sanayi Bolge Mudurlugu, 100. Yil Bulvari No 99, Ostim, Ankara; Tel +90 312 385 5090; Fax +90 312 354 5898; www.ostim.org.tr

Ankara OIZ, Ankara Sanayi Odası I., Organize Sanayi Bölgesi, Ayaş yolu 25. km., 06935 Sincan, Ankara; Tel +90 312 267 0000; Fax +90 312 267 0009; www.aosb.org.tr

Antalya OIZ, Antalya Organize Sanayi, Antalya; Tel +90 242 258 1100; www.antalyaosb.org.tr

Balıkesir OIZ, Balıkesir Organize Sanayi Bölgesi, Savaştepe Karayolunun 7. km, Balıkesir; www.balosb.org.tr

Denizli OIZ, Denizli Organize Sanayi Bölgesi, Gürlek, Honaz, Denizli; Tel +90 258 269 1002; Fax +90 258 269 1001; www.dosb.org.tr

Gaziantep OIZ, Gaziantep Organize Sanayi Bölgesi, Başpınar, Gaziantep; Tel +90 342 337 1101; Fax +90 342 337 1371; www.gaosb.org

Gebze OIZ, Organize Sanayi Bölgesi, Yönetim Merkezi, 41480 Gebze, Kocaeli; Tel +90 262 648 4848; Fax +90 262 648 4822; www.gosb.com.tr

Eskisehir OIZ, Eskişehir Organize Sanayi Bölgesi, 26110 Eskişehir; Tel +90 222 236 0360; Fax +90 222 236 0129; www.eosb.org.tr

Ikitelli (Istanbul) OIZ, Ikitelli Organize Sanayi Bölgesi, Istanbul; www.ikitelliorg.com

Istanbul Dudullu OIZ, Organize Sanayi Bölge Müdürlüğü, Organize Sanayi Bölgesi 4. Caddesi, Yukarı Dudullu Ümraniye, İstanbul; Tel +90 216 365 7403; Fax +90 216 420 4415; www.idosb.org.tr

Aliağa (Izmir) OIZ, Aliağa Organize Bölgesi, Atatürk Cad. N:372/1, Katipoğlu A Blok K:7 D:7, 35220 Alsancak, İzmir; Tel +90 232 463 2394; Fax +90 232 463 3511; www.alosbi.org.tr

Tire (İzmir) OIZ, Tire Organize Sanayi Bölgesi, İzmir; www.tosbi.org.tr

Izmir Atatürk OIZ, Izmir Atatürk Organize Sanayi Bölgesi, Mustafa Kemal Atatürk Bulvarı No 42, 35620 Çiğli, İzmir; Tel +90 232 376 7176; Fax +90 232 376 7100; www.iaosb.org.tr

Kemalpaşa (Izmir) OIZ, Kemalpaşa Organize Sanayi, Ismet Inönü Caddesi No 38 Zemin Kat, Kemalpaşa, Izmir; Tel +90 232 878 8853; Fax +90 232 878 8144; www.kosbi.org.tr

Kayseri OIZ, Kayseri Organize Sanayi Bölgesi, Kayseri; www.kosb.org

Manisa OIZ, Manisa Ticaret ve Sanayi Odası Organize Sanayi Bölgesi, Organize Sanayi Bölgesi, Kurtuluş Caddesi No 2, 45030 Manian; Tel +90 236 233 1816; Fax +90 236 233 2547; www.@mosb.org.tr

Manisa OIZ, Manisa Organize Sanayi Bölgesi, Manisa; www.mtso.org

Trabzon – Arsin OIZ, Organize Sanayi Bölgesi 9. Cad No 2, 61900 Arsin, Trabzon; Tel +90 462 711 3717; Fax +90 462 711 2522; www.tosbol.org.tr

Torbalı I OIZ, Torbalı I Organize Sanayi Bölgesi, Torbalı, İzmir; www.ebso.org.tr/tr/osb/osbmain.php

Torbalı II OIZ, Cumhuriyet Bulvari No 63 K: 3 PK, 35210 Paşaport, Izmir; Tel +90 232 446 5609; Fax +90 232 484 0291; www.ebso.org.tr/tr/osb/osbmain.php

Priority Development Areas

Cities

Adiyaman; Agri; Aksaray; Amasya; Ardahan; Artvin; Bartin; Batman; Bayburt; Bingöl; Bitlis; Çanakkale (Bozcaaada and Gökçeada); Çankiri; Çorum; Diyarbakir; Elazig; Erzincan,; Erzurum; Giresun; Gümüshane; Hakkari; Igdir; Kahramanmaras; Karabük; Karaman; Kars; Kastamonu; Kirikkale; Kirsehir; Kilis; Malatya; Mardin; Mus; Nevsehir; Nigde; Ordu; Osmaniye; Rize; Samsun; Siirt; Sinop; Sivas; Sanliurfa; Sirnak; Tokat; Trabzon; Tunceli; Van; Yozgat; Zonguldak

Provinces

Adiyaman; Afyon; Agri; Aksaray; Amasya; Ardahan; Bartin; Batman; Bayburt; Bingöl; Bitlis; Çankiri; Diyarbakir; Düzce; Erzincan; Erzurum

Giresun; Gümüshane; Hakkari; Igdir; Kars; Kirsehir; Malatya; Mardin; Mus; Ordu; Osmaniye; Siirt; Sinop; Sivas; Sanliurfa; Sirnak; Usak; Van; Yozgat

EXPATRIATE RESOURCES (TURKEY)

Turkish Expat Portal – www.mymerhaba.com

General Expat site with Turkish section – www.expatfocus.com

General Expat site with Turkish section – www.britishexpat.com

General Expat site with Turkish section – www.turkey.alloexpat.com

American Women of Istanbul – www.awi-istanbul.com

TAX AUTHORITY RESOURCES

UK

The Pension Service, International Pensions centre, Tyneview Park, Newcastle Upon Tyne NE98 1BA; Tel +44 191 218 777; Fax +44 191 218 3836; www.dwp.gov.uk

Her Majesty's Revenue and Customs, HMRC Residency, Fitzroy House, P.O.Box 46, Nottingham, United Kingdom NG2 1BD (To apply for UK tax allowances whilst non-resident); Tel 0845 070 0040 (within UK), Tel +44 151 210 2222 (outside the UK); www.hmrc.gov.uk

For specific information on Guardian's Allowance contact HM Revenue and Customs, Child Benefit Office, P.O.Box 1, Washington, Newcastle Upon Tyne NE88 1AA; Tel +44 191 225 1536; Fax +44 191 225 1543; child.benefit@hmrc.gsi.gov.uk

Canada

International Tax Services Office, Canada Revenue Agency, 2204 Walkley Road, Ottawa ON K1A 1A8, Canada; www.cra-arc.gc.ca; calls from Canada and the US 1800 267 5177; calls from outside Canada and the US +1 613 952 3741

International Operations, Service Canada, Ottawa, Ontario K1A
0L4; Tel +1 613 957 1954; Fax +1 613 952 8901; From Canada or
the United States (in English) 1800 454 8731 or TDD 1800 255
4786; www.servicecanada.gc.ca

Australia

Centrelink International Services (GPO Box 273, Hobart TAS 7001,
Australia; Tel 13 1673 (inside Australia); Tel 00 800 6190 5703
(freephone from Turkey); Tel +61 3 6222 3455 (any international
call); Fax +61 3 6222 2799; www.centrelink.gov.au;
international.services@centrelink.gov.au

Australian Tax Office, GPO Box 9990 in the capital city of your
home state/territory; www.ato.gov.au; Tel 13 2861;
International Tel +61 2 6216 1111

New Zealand

New Zealand Superannuation; Tel 0800 552002 (to make an
appointment before leaving the country)

International Services, Work and Income, P.O.Box 27178,
Wellington, New Zealand; Tel +64 4978 1180; Fax +64 4918 0159;
international-services@msd.govt.nz

For assistance with a Veteran Pension contact War Pension Services,
P.O.Box 9448, Hamilton, New Zealand; Free Phone 0800 553 003;
Free Fax 0508 402 402; warpension@msd.govt.nz

Inland Revenue offices (www.ird.govt.nz) and advice lines

Inland Revenue, P.O.Box 1477, Waikato Mail Centre, Hamilton 3240

Inland Revenue, P.O.Box 39010, Wellington Mail Centre, Lower
Hutt 5045

Inland Revenue, P.O.Box 3753, Christchurch Mail Centre,
Christchurch 8140

Telephone call from within New Zealand; 0800 227 774;

Telephone call from outside New Zealand; +64 4 978 0779

USA

Social Security Administration, P.O.Box 17769, Baltimore, Maryland 21235-7769, USA; www.socialsecurity.gov

Internal Revenue Service Center, Austin, TX 73301-0215, USA

Internal Revenue Service by mail at P.O.Box 920, Bensalem, PA 19020, USA; Tel +1 215 516 2000 (not toll-free); Fax +1 215 516 2555; www.irs.gov (for written international enquiries)

Federal Pension Information: www.usa.gov/Agencies/State_and_Territories.shtml/

Consumer Rights Organization (www.pensionrights.org)

Ireland

Collector General (Sarsfield House, Francis Street, Limerick.; Tel 1890 20 30 70 (in Ireland); +353 61 488 000 (International callers); www.revenue.ie; cg@revenue.ie)

HEALTHCARE

National Authorities

UK Department of Health: www.dh.gov.uk

Health Canada: http://hc-sc.gc.ca

New Zealand Ministry of Health: www.moh.govt.nz/eligibility

Australian Department for Health and Ageing: www.health.gov.au

US Medicare: www.medicare.gov

Private Healthcare Providers

Bayindir Hastanesi (24-hour emergency service), Kızılırmak Mahallesi, 28. Sokak, Söğütözü, Ankara; Tel +90 312 287 9000

JFK Hastanesi, Talatpaşa Bulvarı, Begonya Sokak, 7-9, Bahçelievler, Istanbul; Tel +90 212 441 4142

Med American, Cemil Topuzlu Caddesi 46, Çiftehavuzlar, Istanbul; Tel +90 216 478 2555

Acil Yardım ve Trafik Hastanesi (Emergency and Traffic Accident Hospital), Gümüşpala Mahallesi, E-5 Güzergahı, Avcılar, Istanbul; Tel +90 212 591 3416; Fax +90 212 591 2813

International Hastanesi, İstanbul Caddesi, Yeşilköy, Istanbul; Tel +90 212 663 3000; Fax +90 212 663 2862

Güven Hastanesi, Şimşek Sokak 29, Ayrancı, Ankara; Tel +90 312 468 7270

Ahmet Örs Hastanesi, Çiftlik Caddesi, 57 Emek Mahallesi, Emek, Ankara; Tel +90 312 212 6262

Acibadem Hastanesi, Nilufer, Bursa, Tel +90 224 270 4444

Lara Hospital, Havaalani Caddesi Sevinc Sokak No 9, Lara, Antalya; Tel +90 242 349 4040; Fax +90 242 349 2626

Saglik Hastanesi, 1399 Sokak 25, Alsancak, Izmir; Tel +90 232 463 7700

Izmir Hastanesi, Gaziler cad. No 155, Kapilar, Izmir; Tel +90 232 445 2926

MEDLAB, Iran Cad. 13/13, Kavaklidere, Ankara; Tel +90 312 467 1954; Fax +90 312 467 1925

BANKS

State Owned Turkish Banks

T.C. Ziraat Bankasi A.Ş.; www.ziraat.com.tr

Türkiye Halk Bankasi A.Ş.: www.halkbank.com.tr

Türkiye Vakiflar Bankasi A.O.: www.vakifbank.com.tr

Private Turkish Banks

Adabank A.Ş.; www.adabank.com.tr

Akbank T.A.Ş.; www.akbank.com.tr

Alternatif Bank A.Ş.; www.abank.com.tr

Anadolu Bank A.Ş.; www.anadolubank.com.tr

Oyak Bank A.Ş.; www.oyakbank.com.tr

Şekerbank T.A.Ş.; www.sekerbank.com.tr

Tekstil Bankasi A.Ş.; www.tekstilbank.com.tr

Turkish Bank A.Ş.; www.turkishbank.com

Türk Ekonomi Bankasi A.Ş.; www.teb.com.tr

Türkiye Garanti Bankasi A.Ş.; www.garanti.com.tr

Türkiye Iş Bankasi A.Ş.; www.isbank.com.tr

Yapi Ve Kredi Bankasi A.Ş.; www.yapikredi.com.tr

Foreign Owned Banks Operating in Turkey

Arap Türk Banakasi A.Ş.; www.arabturkbank.com

Citibank A.Ş.; www.citibank.com.tr

Denizbank A.Ş.; www.denizbank.com

Deutsche Bank A.Ş.; www.deutschebank.com.tr

Finansbank A.Ş.; www.finansbank.com.tr

Fortis Bank A.Ş.; www.fortis.com.tr

HSBC Bank A.Ş.; www.hsbc.com.tr

Millennium Bank A.Ş.; www.millenniumbank.com.tr

Tekfenbank A.Ş.; www.tekfenbank.com.tr

Turkland Bank A.Ş.; www.turklandbank.com

Turkish Insurance Companies

*Acıbadem Sağlık ve Hayat Sigorta A.Ş.:
www.acibademsigorta.com.tr

*Aksigorta A.Ş.; www.aksigorta.com.tr

*Aig Sigorta A.Ş.; www.aig.com

*American Life Hayat Sigorta A.Ş.; www.alico-measa.com

214

*Anadolu Anonim Türk Sigorta Şirketi; www.anadolusigorta.com.tr

Anadolu Hayat Emeklilik A.Ş.; www.anadoluhayat.com.tr

*Ankara Anonim Türk Sigorta Şirketi; www.ankarasigorta.com.tr

Ankara Emeklilik A.Ş.; www.ankaraemeklilik.com.tr

*Axa Oyak Sigorta A.Ş.; www.axaoyaksigorta.com.tr

*Axa Oyak Hayat Sigorta A.Ş.; www.axaoyak.com.tr

Aviva Sigorta A.Ş.; www.avivasigorta.com.tr

AvivaSa Hayat ve Emeklilik A.Ş.; www.aviva.com.tr

Atradius Credit Insurance N.V. Türkiye İstanbul Şubesi;
http://global.atradius.com/

*Başak Sigorta A.Ş.; www.basak.com.tr

Başak Groupama Emeklilik A.Ş.; www.basakemeklilik.com.tr

*Batı Sigorta A.Ş.; www.batisigorta.com.tr

*Birlik Sigorta A.Ş.; www.birliksigorta.com.tr

Birlik Hayat Sigorta A.Ş.; www.birlikhayatsigorta.com.tr

Cardif Hayat Sigorta A.Ş.; www.cardif.com.tr

Cardif Sigorta A.Ş.; www.cardif.com.tr

Coface Sigorta A.Ş.; www.coface.com

Demir Sigorta A.Ş.; www.demirsigorta.com.tr

*Demir Hayat Sigorta A.Ş.; www.demirhayat.com.tr

Eureko Sigorta A.Ş.; www.garanti-sigorta.com.tr

Fortis Emeklilik ve Hayat A.Ş.; www.fortisemeklilik.com.tr

Fiba Sigorta A.Ş.; www.finanssigorta.com.tr

*Garanti Emeklilik ve Hayat A.Ş.; www.garantiemeklilik.com.tr

*Genel Yaşam Sigorta A.Ş.; www.genelyasam.com.tr

*Generali Sigorta A.Ş.; www.generali.com.tr

Global Hayat Sigorta A.Ş.; www.globalhayat.com.tr

*Güneş Sigorta A.Ş.; www.gunessigorta.com.tr

*Güven Sigorta T.A.Ş.; www.guvensigorta.com.tr

*Güven Hayat Sigorta A.Ş.; www.guvenhayat.com.tr

Hür Sigorta A.Ş.; www.hursigorta.com.tr

Inter Sigorta A.Ş

*Işık Sigorta A.Ş.; www.isiksigorta.com

Hdi Sigorta A.Ş.; www.hdisigorta.com.tr

Ergoisviçre Sigorta A.Ş.; www.ergoisvicre.com.tr

Ergoisviçre Hayat Sigorta A.Ş.; www.isvicrehayat.com.tr

*Koç Allianz Sigorta A.Ş.; www.kocallianz.com.tr

Koç Allianz Hayat ve Emeklilik A.Ş.; www.kocallianz.com.tr

Liberty Sigorta A.Ş.; www.libertysigorta.com.tr

Magdeburger Sigorta A.Ş

Merkez Sigorta A.Ş.; www.merkezsigorta.com

New Life Yaşam Sigorta A.Ş.; www.nly.com.tr

*Ray Sigorta A.Ş.; www.raysigorta.com.tr

Rumeli Sigorta A.Ş

Rumeli Hayat Sigorta A.Ş

Teb Sigorta A.Ş.; www.tebsigorta.com.tr

*Ticaret Sigorta A.Ş.; www.ticaretsigorta.com.tr

*T.Genel Sigorta A.Ş.; www.genelsigorta.com

Türk Nippon Sigorta A.Ş.; www.turknippon.com.tr

Toprak Sigorta A.Ş.; www.topraksigorta.com.tr

Vakıf Emeklilik A.Ş.; www.vakifemeklilik.com.tr

*Yapı Kredi Sigorta A.Ş.; www.yksigorta.com.tr

Yapı Kredi Emeklilik A.Ş.; www.ykemeklilik.com

* – also offer health insurance

Offshore Banks

NatWest International Personal Banking, P.O.Box 554, 16 Library Place, St Helier, Jersey JE4 8NH, Channel Islands; Tel +44 1534 282 300; Fax +44 1534 285 616; www.natwestinternational.com

HSBC Bank International Limited, HSBC House, Esplanade, St Helier, Jersey JE1 1HS, Channel Islands; Tel +44 1534 616 111; www.offshore.hsbc.com

Lloyds TSB Offshore, Broad Street, P.O.Box 10, 9 Broad Street, St. Helier, Jersey, JE4 8NG; Tel +44 8457 309 461; Fax +44 1534 284 644; www.lloydstsb-offshore.com

Lloyds TSB Offshore Limited, International Personal Banking, One Biscayne Towers, Suite 3200, 2 South Biscayne Boulevard, Miami, FL 33131, Florida, USA; Tel +1 305 347 7140; Fax +1 305 371 8607; internationalbanking@lloydstsb-usa.com; www.lloydstsb-usa.com

Royal Bank of Scotland International, P.O.Box 64, 71 Bath Street, St Helier, Jersey, Channel Islands JE4 8PJ; Tel +44 1534 285 200; Fax +44 1534 285 588; www.rbsint.com

Allied Irish Bank Offshore, AIB Bank (CI) Limited, AIB House, 25 Esplanade, St. Helier, Jersey JE1 2AB; Tel +44 1624 639 772; www.alliedirishoffshore.com

Citibank N.A., P.O.Box 561, 38 Esplanade, St Helier, Jersey JE4 5WQ, Channel Islands; Tel +44 1534 608 020; Fax +44 1534 608 390; www.citibank.com

Griffon Bank, P.O.Box 1324, Roseau, Commonwealth of Dominica, West Indies; Tel +1 767 449 9254; www.griffonbank.com

UBS (Bahamas) Ltd., UBS House, East Bay Street, Nassau, Bahamas; Tel +1 242 394 9300; Fax +1 242 394 9333; www.ubs.com

Royal Bank of Canada (Channel Islands) Limited, P.O.Box 194, 19-21 Broad Street, St Helier, Jersey, Channel Islands JE4 8RR; Tel +44 1534 283 838; Fax +44 1534 283 926; www.rbcprivatebanking.com

INLAND TRANSPORT

Local Metro Transport Options

Ankara Metro; www.ankarametrosu.com.tr

Ankaray; www.ankaray.com.tr

Istanbul Transportation Company (Istanbul Ulaşım Transportation Co.); www.istanbul-ulasim.com.tr/en/

Izmir's Metro; www.izmirmetro.com.tr

Istanbul Tramway; www.dersaadettramvayi.com

Ferry Services

Istanbul Deniz Otobüsleri; www.ido.com.tr/en/

TURYOL (Istanbul); www.turyol.com.tr

DenizLine; www.denizline.com.tr

Izmir Denizcilic Işletmeleri; www.izdeniz.com.tr

Domestic Flights

Turkish Airlines (Türk Hava Yolları, THY); www.thy.com.tr

Sun Express; www.sunexpress.de

Izair; www.izair.com.tr

AtlasJet; www.atlasjet.com

OnurAir; www.onurair.com.tr

Long Distance Bus Operators

Asya Tur; www.asyatur.com.tr

Istanbul Seyahat; www.istanbulseyahat.com.tr

Kamil Koç; www.kamilkoc.com.tr

Metro Turizm; www.metroturizm.com.tr

Pamukkale Seyahat; www.pamukkaleturizm.com.tr

Ulusoy; www.ulusoy.com.tr

Varan; www.varan.com.tr/english/

The Fez Bus; www.feztravel.com

Train Travel

Turkish State Railways (Türkiye Cumhuriyeti Devlet Demiryollari, TCDD); www.tcdd.gov.tr

Bus Terminals

Esenler Otobüs Terminalı (Büyük Otogar, European side of Istanbul); Tel +90 212 658 0036; www.otogaristanbul.com

Harem Terminal (Üsküdar, Asian side of Istanbul); Tel +90 216 333 3763

AŞTİ Terminal (Ankara); Tel +90 312 224 1000; www.asti.com.tr

INTERNATIONAL TRANSPORT

Turkish Airports and Airports Information Sites

General Directorate of State Airports Authority (Devlet Hava Meydanları İşletmesi); www.dhmi.gov.tr/newenglish/index.asp

Istanbul Atatürk Airport; www.ataturkairport.com

Ankara Esenboğa Airport; www.ataturkairport.com/esb/esben/

Izmir Adnan Menderes Airport; www.adnanmenderesairport.com

Antalya Airport International Terminal; www.antaliaairport.com

Muğla-Dalaman; www.atmairport.aero

Airports Wordwide; www.airports-worldwide.com

Skytrax; www.airlinequality.com

Online Ticket Agents

www.opodo.com

www.ebookers.com

www.flights.com

www.cheapflights.com

www.orbitz.com

Airlines Flying to Turkey

Türk Hava Yolları; www.thy.com

American Airlines (New York, Chicago); www.aa.com

Delta Airlines (New York); www.delta.com

United Airlines (via Dusseldorf and Munich); www.united.com

Continental Airlines (via Amsterdam); www.continental.com

NorthWest Airlines (via Amsterdam and Paris); www.nwa.com

US Airways (via Frankfurt and Munich); www.usairways.com

Lufthansa (via Munich, Frankfurt and Dusseldorf);
www.lufthansa.com

Alitalia (Rome, Milan); www.alitalia.com

Swiss International Airlines (Zurich); www.swiss.com

KLM (Amsterdam); www.klm.com

Air France (Paris); www.airfrance.com

Iberia (Madrid); www.iberia.com

British Airways (Heathrow); www.ba.com

Easy Jet (Gatwick and Luton); www.easyjet.com

Singapore Airlines (Singapore); www.singaporeair.com

Ferry Services to Turkey

Italy – Turkey

Operator: Marmara Lines; www.marmaralines.com

Brindisi – Çeşme

Ancona – Çeşme

Ukraine – Turkey

Operator: UKR Ferry Shiping Company; www.ukrferry.com

Ilyichevsk (Ukraine) – Derince (Turkey)

Odessa (Ukraine) – Istanbul (Turkey)

Northern Cyprus – Turkey

Operator: Fergün Shipping – http://fergun.net/uk/index.htm

    Girne – Alanya

    Taşuçu – Girne

Operator: Akgünler Shipping; www.akgunler.com.tr/english.htm

    Mersin – Famagusta

Greek Islands – Turkey

    Lesvos – Ayvalik

    Samos – Kuşadaşi

    Kos – Bodrum

    Chios – Çeşme

    Simi – Datça

    Rhodes – Fethiye

    Rhodes – Bodrum

    Rhodes – Marmaris

International Train Services and Information

    InterRail; www.interrail.com

    Iranian Railways; www.rajatrains.com/indexe.asp

    Syrian Railways; www.cfssyria.org

    Thomas Cook Publishing (train timetables); www.thomascookpublishing.com

LEISURE

Leisure Resources

Turkish Golf Federation (BJK Plaza No 92 A Blok No 1-4, 80690 Beşiktaş, Istanbul; Tel +90 212 258 0718; Fax +90 212 236 8304; www.tgf.org.tr

Kemer Golf and Country Club, Goktür Köyü, Uzun Kemer Mevkii Kemerburgaz, Istanbul; +90 212 239 7010; www.kg-cc.com

Klassis Golf and Country Club, Seymen Köyü, Altıntepe Mevkii, 34930 Silivri, Istanbul; Tel +90 212 710 1300; www.klassisgolf.com.tr

Turkish Golf; www.turkishgolf.com

Golf International Friendship Society Golf Sports Club, TGIF Golf Sports Club, Ahlatlibel Golf Tesisleri, Ahlatlibel, Anakra; Tel +90 312 491 2119; www.tgifgolf.com

TurkeyandGolf.com; www.golf.com.tr

The Lycian Way; www.lycianway.com

St Paul's Trail; www.stpaultrail.com

Turkish Association of Spas, Thalasso and Health Resorts (TURKSPA), Millet Caddesi 126, 34390 Istanbul; Tel +90 532 477 6965; mzkaragulle@tnn.net; www.spaturkey.com

Antalya Golden Orange Film Festival – http://altinportakal.tursak.org.tr/indexen.php

Istanbul Film Festival; www.istanbulfilmfestival.com

Ankara International Film Festival; www.filmfestankara.org.tr

Sports International; www.sportsinternational.com.tr

Ankara – Bilkent 1. Cadde, Bilkent, Ankara; Tel +90 312 266 7100; Fax +90 312 266 7123

Ataköy Sports International, Ataköy Marina, Sahilyolu 34710, Ataköy, Istanbul; Tel +90 212 559 3333; Fax +90 212 661 2212

Şişli Sports International, 19 Mayıs Cad., Dr.İsmet Öztürk Sok. No 17, 80220 Şişli, Istanbul; Tel +90 212 296 2515; Fax +90 212 248 3315

Kadıköy Sports International, Tepe Nautilus Alışveriş Merkezi Fatih Cad. No 1, Acıbadem 34650, Kadıköy, Istanbul; Tel +90 216 339 2500; Fax +90 216 339 7704

Izmir Sports International, 2040 Sok. No 3 Mavişehir, 35540 Karşıyaka, Izmir; Tel +90 232 324 1500; Fax +90 232 324 1510

Kavaklidere Wines; www.kavaklidere.com

Pammukkale Wines; www.pamukkalesarap.com

Selected Hunting Tour Operators

Turban Tourism, Karanfil Sok. No 32, Kızılay, Ankara; Tel +90 312 419 5151; Fax +90 312 419 5154

Antalya Capra Hunting & Fishing & Travelling, Yeşilbahçe Mah., Portakal Çiçeği Bulvarı, M.N. Yiğitbaşı Apt. No 45/2, Antalya; Tel +90 242 312 2123; Fax +90 242 312 2125

Turkuaz Tourism, Türkmen Mah., Birlik Yapı Sitesi Nilüfer sok. No 1/1, Kuşadası; Tel +90 256 618 1519; Fax +90 256 618 1522

Gemini Tourism, Barboros Bulvarı, Günaydın-2 Apt. 131/3-4, Balmumcu, Beşiktaş; Tel +90 212 275 3384; Fax +90 212 275 3386

Turkuaz Tur Tourism, Beşkuyular Mevkii, BP Yıkama Servisi Karşısı, Konacık, Bodrum; Tel +90 317 1420; Fax +90 252 317 1440

Camping Club Europe; www.campingclubeurope.com

Eurocamping (also sells a DVD directory of European camp-sites); www.eurocampings.co.uk

Popular Spa Resort Locations

Kizilçahamam, Ayas & Haymana (near Ankara)

Çekirge (near Bursa)

Pamukkale (near Denizli)

Çesme (near Izmir)

Kangal (near Sivas)

Yalova Termal (near Yalova)

Leisure Providers and Organisations

Department of Youth and Sports Turkish Mountaineering Federation, Ulus, Ankara; Tel +90 312 310 1578; Fax +90 312 310 1578

IAH Holiday Walking Ltd, P.O.Box 59, Ruardean, Gloucestershire GL17 9WX, UK; Tel +44 871 855 2925; Fax +44 871 855 2929; Skype – flightholiday; www.holidaywalking.co.uk

F Holidays Limited, Catalyst House, 720 Centennial Court, Centennial Park, Elstree, Hertfordshire WD6 3SY, UK; Tel +44 20 8732 1220; Fax +44 20 8732 1240; www.hfholidays.co.uk

ANZAC Guide Turkey; www.anzacguide.com

Samistal Travel, Istasyon Caddesi, Çeşmeli Sokak No 10, 51100 Niğde; Tel +90 388 232 9151; Fax +90 388 232 9152; Mobile +90 533 259 68 84; www.samistaltravel.com

Middle Earth Travel, Gaferli Mah. Cevizler Sok. No 20 50180 Goreme – Nevsehir / Turkey; Tel +90 384 271 2559; Fax. +90 384 271 2562; www.middleearthtravel.com

Vinotolia, Husrev Gerede cad., Zumrutsaray ap. No 11 Daire: 17, 80200 Tesvikiye, Istanbul; Tel +90 212 261 5169; Mobile +90 532 266 7697; www.vinotolia.com (run wine courses in Cappadocia)

Hugh and Jane, Guided tours of Turkey; Tel + 44 1962 865345; Fax + 44 1962 865345; Mobile + 44 7802 871927; www.hughandjane.co.uk

MOVING

Freight Forwarding Resources

British International Freight Forwarders Association, Redfern House, Browells Lane, Feltham, Middlesex. TW13 7EP; Tel +44 20 8844 2266; Fax +44 20 8890 5546; bifa@bifa.org; www.bifa.org

European Freight Forwarders Association; www.effa.com

Canadian International Freight Forwarders Association, 170 Attwell Drive, Suite 480, Toronto, Ontario M9W 5Z5; Tel +1 416 234 5100; Toll Free in Canada: 1 866 282 4332; Fax +1 416 234 5152; www.ciffa.com

Freight Forwarder, Logistics and Cargo Directory

www.freightnet.com

Removal Companies

International Federation of Removal Companies (Fédération Internationale des Déménageurs Internationaux, FIDI aisbl), 69 Rue Picard B-5, 1080 Brussels, Belgium; Tel +32 2426 5160; Fax +32 2426 5523; http://fidi.com

European Relocation Association, P.O.Box 189, Diss IP22 1PE, UK; Tel +44 8700 726727; Fax +44 1379 641940; www.eura-relocation.com

British Association of Removers, Tangent House, 62 Exchange Road, Watford, Hertfordshire WD18 0TG; Tel +44 192 369 9480; Fax +44 192 369 9481; www.bar.co.uk

Pet Relocation Agents and Associations

International Pet and Animal Transport Association, 745 Winding Trail, Holly Lake Ranch, Texas 75755, USA; Tel +1 903 769 2267; Fax +1 903 769 28671 www.ipata.com

Pet Travel Services, 24 Couston Street, Dunfermline, KY12 7QW, Scotland; Tel +44 138 372 2819; Fax +44 138 373 0787; info@pettravelservices.co.uk; www.pettravelservices.co.uk

Alrona Kennel/Cattery & Pet Transporters, Kaitoke Loop, Kaitoke, Upper Hutt, New Zealand, Tel +64 4 526 7348; Fax :+64 4 526 7348; info@alrona.co.nz; www.alrona.co.nz

Worldwide Animal Travel, Richmond, British Columbia (BC), Canada; Tel +1 604 303 7384; Fax +1 604 303 7354; +1 866 302 6688 (toll-free, Canada only); pets@animaltravel.com; www.animaltravel.com

Boomerang Pet Carrier, Suite 142, 919 Centre Street N., Calgary, Alberta, Canada T2E 2P6; Tel +1 403 803 9750; Fax +1 403 276 1877; boomerang@shaw.ca; www.boomerangpetcarrier.com

Ferndale Kennels. SX-2031 Pak Tam Chung, Sai Kung Country Park, Hong Kong; Tel +852 2791 9330; Fax +852 2792 4340; shipping@ferndalekennels.com; www.ferndalekennels.com

Breeny Boarding and Quarantine Kennels, Belfast, Co. Down, North Ireland, UK; Tel +44 289 040 2068; Fax +44 289 040 3880; lisnabreenypets@aol.com; www.breenypets.co.uk

Animals Away (USA); Toll-free 1 800 492 7961; www.animalsaway.com

JetPets Inc, 9111 Falmouth Ave, Playa Del Rey, CA 90293-8617, USA; Tel +1 310 823 8901; Fax +1 310 305 8297; Continental USA 1-800 PET-8901; www.jetpets.com

Pet Relocation & Services, Spicewood, Texas (TX), United States; Tel +1 512 264 9800; Fax +1 512 264 9808; USA Toll Free +1 877-Pet-Move (877 738 6683); info@petrelocation.com; www.petrelocation.com

Ozdoggy, P.O.Box 333, Warburton, VIC 3799, Australia; Tel +61 3 409 004 770; www.ozdoggy.com.au

JET PETS, 64 Lambeck Drive, Tullamarine, VIC 3043, Australia; Tel +61 3 9339 4300; Australia Wide 1300 668 309; Fax +61 3 9335 1206; www.jetpets.com.au

Pets Transport, Lot 3, Sixth Road, Berkshire Park NSW 2765; Tel +61 2 4777 4746; Mobile +61 411 681 394; www.petstransport.com.au

International Driving Permit Issuers

The Royal Automobile Club (UK) – Applications can be made by post using a form downloaded from: www.rac.co.uk

The Automobile Association (UK) – Applications can be made in person at many UK post offices or by post using a form downloaded from: www.theaa.com

American Automobile Club (USA) – Applications can be made in person at any AAA office or by post using a form downloaded from: www.aaa.com/vacation/idpf.html

Royal Automobile Club of Queensland (Australia) – Applications can be made in person at any RACQ office or by post using a form downloaded from: www.racq.com.au

Royal Automobile Club of Western Australia (Australia) – Applications can be made in person at any RAC WA office or by post using a form downloaded from: http://rac.com.au

Canadian Automobile Club – Applications can be made in person at any CAC office, provincial association office, or by post using a form downloaded from: www.caa.ca

New Zealand Automobile Association – Applications can be made in person at any AA Centre or AA Driver and Vehicle Licensing Agent, or by post using a form downloaded from: www.aa.co.nz

Automobile Association Ireland – Applications can be made by post to AA, 56 Drury Street, Dublin 2, by calling +353 1 617 9999, or by printing an application form from www.aaireland.ie and returning with payment to the above address

The International Motor Club (International) – Online application can be made for the issue of an International Driver's Permit for all nationalities of license except those from the USA: www.internationalmotorclub.org.

Appendix B

BOOKS ON TURKEY

Turkey (Lonely Planet Country Guide), Verity Campbell; Lonely Planet Publications, 1 April 2007; ISBN-10: 1741045568

The Rough Guide to Turkey; Marc S. Dubin, Rough Guides Ltd, 25 Jan 2007; ISBN-10: 1843536064

Turkey (Eyewitness Travel Guides); Suzanne Swan, Dorling Kindersley Publishers Ltd, 1 Feb 2008; ISBN-10: 1405327758

The Turks Today: Turkey After Ataturk; Andrew Mango, John Murray, 11 April 2005; ISBN-10: 0719565952

The Turks in World History; Carter Vaughan Findley, Oxford University Press Inc USA, 13 Jan 2005; ISBN-10: 0195177266

Ataturk; Andrew Mango, John Murray; 16 Feb 2004; ISBN-10: 0719565928

Ataturk: The Rebirth of a Nation, John Balfour Kinross, Weidenfeld & Nicolson History; 15 Nov 2001, ISBN-10: 1842125990

The Ottoman Centuries: The Rise and Fall of the Turkish Empire, Patrick Balfour Kinross, William Morrow, 31 Dec 1979, ISBN-10: 0688080936

Turkish (Lonely Planet Phrasebook); Arzu Kurklu, Lonely Planet Publications, 1 Sep 2005; ISBN-10: 1864503165

Eat Smart in Turkey: How to Decipher the Menu, Know the Market Foods and Embark on a Tasting Adventure; Joan Peterson; Ginkgo Press Inc. Jan 2005, ISBN-10: 096411688X

BOOKS BY TURKISH AUTHORS

Portrait of a Turkish Family, Irfan Orga, Eland Publishing Ltd; 31 Jul 2002, ISBN-10: 0907871828

Young Turk: A Novel in 13 Fragments, Moris Farhi, Saqi Books, 16 Feb 2004, ISBN-10: 0863563511

The Flea Palace, Elif Shafak, Marion Boyars Publishers Ltd; 18 Jun 2005, ISBN-10: 0714531200

The Gaze, Elif Shafak, Marion Boyars Publishers Ltd, 17 May 2006, ISBN-10: 0714531219

Istanbul: Memories of a City, Orhan Pamuk, Faber and Faber, 6 April 2006, ISBN-10: 0571218334

The Black Book, Orhan Pamuk, Faber and Faber; 3 Aug 2006, ISBN-10: 057122525X

The White Castle, Orhan Pamuk, Faber and Faber; 20 Aug 2001, ISBN-10: 0571164668

Memed, My Hawk (Panther) Yasar Kemal, The Harvill Press; 6 Nov 1997, ISBN-10: 1860463916

TURKISH FILMS

Gallipoli (Jeremy Irons, Sam Neill)

Hamam (The Turkish Bath), Director – Ferzan Ozpetek

Uzak, Director – Bilge Nuri Ceylan

Climates, Director – Nuri Bilge Ceylan and Ebru Ceylan

Ararat, Director – Atom Egoyan

Index